NORTON ANTHOLOGY OF *Western Music*

THIRD EDITION

VOLUME *1*

Ancient to Baroque

NORTON ANTHOLOGY OF

Western Music

THIRD EDITION

EDITED BY

CLAUDE V. PALISCA

Yale University

VOLUME *1*

Ancient to Baroque

W · W · NORTON & COMPANY · NEW YORK · LONDON

The text of this book is composed in Bembo, with the display set in Shelley Andante.
Composition by TSI Graphics, Inc.
Book design by Jack Meserole.
Cover art: *Lute with Molecules,* serigraph by Ben Shahn. Courtesy of the Israel Museum,
    Jerusalem. © 1996 Estate of Ben Shahn / Licensed by VAGA, New York, NY.
Cover design by Linda Kosarin.
Title page art: Detail from cover art by Pablo Picasso for Igor Stravinsky's *Ragtime* (London:
    J. & W. Chester, 1919). © 1996 Estate of Pablo Picasso / Artists Rights Society (ARS).
    New York.

ISBN 0-393-96906-1 (pbk.)

W. W. Norton & Company, Inc., 500 Fifth Avenue, New York, N.Y. 10110 http://web.wwnorton.com
W. W. Norton & Company, Ltd., 10 Coptic Street, London WC1A 1PU

4   5   6   7   8   9   0

Contents

The Beginnings of Polyphony and the Music of the Thirteenth Century

French and Italian Music in the Fourteenth Century

England and the Burgundian Lands in the Fifteenth Century

The Age of the Renaissance: Music of the Low Countries

New Currents in the Sixteenth Century

Church Music of the Late Renaissance and Reformation

Music of the Early Baroque Period

Opera and Vocal Music in the Late Seventeenth Century

Instrumental Music in the Late Baroque Period

Music in the Early Eighteenth Century

Appendixes and Indexes

PREFACE

The title *Norton Anthology of Western Music* (NAWM) lacks one important qualifier: it is a *historical* anthology of Western music. There is a wide difference between a historical anthology and one intended to supply a selection of music for study and analysis.

Historians cannot confine themselves to studying in splendid isolation the great works that are the usual stuff of anthologies. They are interested in products of the imagination, great and small, as those exist in a continuum of such works. Just as composers did not create in a musical void, standing aloof from the models of their predecessors and contemporaries, so the historically oriented student and analyst must have the primary material that permits establishing historical connections. This anthology invites students and teachers to make such connections. It confronts, for example, important works and their models—pieces written on a common subject or built according to similar procedures, or that give evidence of subtle influences of one composer's work on another's.

Most music before 1500 was composed on some preexistent music, and there are numerous examples of this practice even after that. Whenever possible in this anthology, the music that served to ignite a composer's imagination is provided. In one notable case a single chant, *Alleluia Pascha nostrum* (NAWM 16), gave rise to a chain of polyphonic elaborations. It was elaborated by Léonin in organum purum with clausulae and refreshed with substitute clausulae by his successors. Anonymous musicians then turned some of the clausulae themselves into motets by fitting them with Latin or French texts or made them fuller by adding new parts, both with and without texts. The Alleluia group in this third edition has been abridged and made to conform to the accompanying recording both in the succession of works and in their manner of notation. (Our Alleluia set, although different in content, format, and realization, is modeled on similar sets based on this chant that were compiled by Richard Crocker and Karl Kroeger as local teaching aids, and I am indebted to them for the general idea and for certain details.)

We may also observe how Josquin in his early motet *Tu solus, qui facis mirabilia* (NAWM 33) absorbed fragments of Ockeghem's arrangement of the song *D'ung aultre amer* (NAWM 31). The process of coloration and variation that produced Luys de Narváez's arrangement for vihuela of Josquin's *Mille regretz* (NAWM 32b) may be inferred by comparing it to the original polyphonic chanson (NAWM 32a). Later examples of this process may be found in the *Pavana Lachrymae* of Byrd (NAWM 47), which is based on Dowland's monodic *Flow, my tears* (NAWM 45), and in George Rochberg's *Nach Bach* (NAWM 152), which is modeled on the Toccata of J. S. Bach's Partita No. 6. In the twentieth century the variation procedure is the structural principle for other excerpts, namely those by Strauss (NAWM 127), Schoenberg (NAWM 139), and Copland (NAWM 145).

Subtler connections may be detected between Musorgsky's song *Okonchen prazdnyi* (NAWM 128) and Debussy's *Nuages* (NAWM 131). If we compare how the same dramatic moments in the legend of Orpheus were realized by Peri and Monteverdi (NAWM 55 and 56), the latter's debts to the former become apparent.

Some of the selections betray foreign influences—for example, the penetration of Italian styles in England, as in Purcell's song from the *Fairy Queen* (NAWM 72), and in Germany, as in the aria from Hasse's *Cleofide* (NAWM 88). A crisis in Handel's career was brought on by the popularity of the ballad opera, exemplified by a scene from *The Beggar's Opera* (NAWM 90) and the English audience's rejection of his own type of Italian *opera seria*. An important stimulus both to Handel and Hasse (NAWM 88) was the new Italian style represented by Pergolesi's *La serva padrona* (NAWM 87).

Several selections document the influence of vernacular and traditional music on art music. Haydn based the finale of his Symphony No. 104 (NAWM 99) on what was probably a Croatian song. Debussy adapted a texture and melodic idiom of the Javanese gamelan to his own orchestral idiom in *Nuages* (NAWM 131). Stravinsky simulated folk-polyphony in the *Le Sacre du printemps* (NAWM 137). Bartók emulated the styles of Serbo-Croatian *parlando-rubato* chanting and of Bulgarian dance orchestras in his *Music for Strings, Percussion, and Celesta* (NAWM 133), and Gunther Schuller caught the flavors of Middle Eastern music in *Arabische Stadt* (NAWM 150b). William Grant Still in his *Afro-American Symphony* (NAWM 146) and Schuller in his *Der Blauteufel* (NAWM 150a) applied elements of the blues and jazz.

Some composers are represented by more than one work to permit comparison of early and late styles (for example, Josquin, Monteverdi, Bach, Vivaldi, Haydn, Beethoven, and Schoenberg) or to show distinct approaches by a single composer to diverse genres (Machaut, Dufay, Victoria, Byrd, Purcell, Buxtehude, Handel, Haydn, Mozart, Beethoven, and Schumann).

A number of the pieces represented new departures in their day—for example, Willaert's *Aspro core* from his *Musica nova* (NAWM 38), Viadana's solo concerto, *O Domine Jesu Christe* (NAWM 62), Rousseau's scene from *Le Devin du village* (NAWM 89), and C. P. E. Bach's sonata (NAWM 94).

Certain pieces won a place because they were singled out by contemporary critics. On the one hand, Arcadelt's *Ahime, dov'è 'l bel viso* (NAWM 37) was hailed in 1549 by Bernardino Cirillo as a ray of hope for the future of text-expressive music; on the other, Monteverdi's *Cruda Amarilli* (NAWM 41) was dismembered by Artusi in his dialogue of 1600 that is at once a critique and a defense of Monteverdi's innovations. Caccini mentioned in the preface to his own *Euridice* that *Perfidissimo volto* (NAWM 54) was one of his pioneering attempts, and Cesti's *Intorno all'idol mio* (NAWM 58) was one of the most frequently cited arias of the mid-seventeenth century. Other works discussed in contemporaneous literature are Lully's monologue in *Armide*, *Enfin il est en ma puissance* (NAWM 70), which was roundly criticized by Rousseau and carefully analyzed by Rameau and d'Alembert; the scene of Carissimi's *Jephte* (NAWM 64), chosen by Athanasius Kircher as a triumph of the powers of musical expression; the first movement of Beethoven's *Eroica* Symphony (NAWM 106) and the *Danse des adolescentes* in Stravinsky's *Le Sacre* (NAWM 137), both objects of critical uproar after their premieres. All these compositions are exemplars of "reception history," a field that has attracted considerable attention recently among teachers and historians.

Certain items serve to correct commonplace misconceptions about the history of music. Cavalieri's *Dalle più alte sfere* (NAWM 53) of 1589 shows that florid monody existed well before 1600. The symphonic movements of Sammartini and Stamitz (NAWM 87 and 95) show that there was more than one path—Haydn's—to the Viennese symphony. The Allegro from Johann Christian Bach's E-flat Harpsichord/Pianoforte Concerto (NAWM 96) testifies to Mozart's dependence on this earlier model in his own Piano Concerto K. 488 (NAWM 102). The movement from Clementi's sonata (NAWM 105) reveals an intense romanticism and creative use of the piano that surpass Beethoven's writing of the same period and probably influenced it.

In keeping with the recent interest in the work of women composers, this anthology has been enriched to include music by Hildegard of Bingen, Comtessa Beatriz de Dia, Barbara Strozzi, Clara Wieck Schumann, Sofia Gubaidulina, and Ruth Crawford Seeger (NAWM 6, 10, 60, 118, 134, and 144).

In general, the selections are free of any insinuations on the part of this editor. They are simply superlative creations that represent their makers, genres, or times. Most of the *ars nova* and many of the Renaissance works fall into this category, as do a majority of those of the Baroque, Romantic, and modern periods. My choices often mark important turning points and shifts of style, historical phenomena that are interesting if not always productive of great music, new models of constructive procedures, typical moments in the work of individual composers, and challenging specimens for historical and structural analysis.

The proportion of space assigned to a person or work does not reflect my valuation of the composer's greatness. Regrettably, many major figures could not be represented at all. In an anthology of limited size every work chosen excludes another of corresponding size that may be equally worthy. Didactic functionality, historical illumination, and intrinsic musical quality, rather than "greatness," "genius," or popularity, were the major criteria for selection.

The inclusion of a complete Office (NAWM 4) and a nearly complete Mass (NAWM 3) deserves special comment. I realize that the rituals as represented here have little validity as historical documents of the Middle Ages.

It would have been more authentic, perhaps, to present a Mass and Office as practiced in a particular place at a particular moment, say in the twelfth century. Since the Vatican Council, the liturgies printed here are themselves archaic formulas, but that fact strengthens the case for their inclusion, because opportunities to experience a Vespers service or Mass sung in Latin in their classic formulations are now rare indeed. I decided to reproduce the editions of the modern chant books, with their stylized neumatic notation, despite the fact that they are not *Urtexte,* because these books are the only resources many students will have available for this repertory, and it should be part of their training to become familiar with the editorial conventions of the Solesmes editions.

Many of the recordings that accompany this anthology are new to this edition. I have taken advantage, other factors being equal, of the improved fidelity of digital recording. I was partly guided in the choices for early music by recent published opinion about performance practices. For the Baroque and early Classic periods, I have favored ensembles that use period instruments. Although the extension of this practice to later music is still controversial, I have included very attractive renditions with period instruments of the excerpts from the symphonies of Beethoven and Berlioz, in part to stimulate discussion and consideration of this option. Users of our recorded anthology should keep in mind that performers take liberties with written scores, and students should not expect to hear every notated detail. This is particularly true with respect to musica ficta, where the editor may have suggested one solution and the performers chosen another, and in periods and genres of music in which improvisation and embellishment by the artists were expected. Compact-disk track numbers have been added (in square boxes) to the scores, and they are placed not only at the beginning but strategically within selections to aid in study, analysis, and teaching.

The third edition of this anthology and the fifth edition of *A History of Western Music* (HWM), for which it serves as a resource, depart from previous editions in that commentaries and analytical notes concerning the selections are being published in NAWM and largely omitted from HWM. However, very brief discussions and more extended treatments of some pieces have been retained in HWM, because they serve to make concrete some of the general trends and techniques considered under each topic. This edition departs from the previous two also in that the selections have been arranged in the order in which they are discussed in HWM rather than by period and genre. An index of references to the numbers of this anthology in HWM appears at the back of each volume.

Although this anthology was conceived as a companion to HWM, it is also intended to stand by itself as a selection of music representing major trends, genres, national schools, and historical developments or innovations.

The poetic and prose texts that appear just following many vocal works are given in the most accurate versions available; no attempt has been made to make the underlaid texts conform to these readings. The translations of the foreign texts are my own, except where acknowledged. They are literal to a fault, corresponding to the original line by line, if not word for word, with consequent inevitable damage to the English style. In my experience, the music analyst prefers precise detail concerning the composer's text to imaginative and evocative writing. I am indebted to Ann Walters Robertson for helping with some stubborn medieval Latin poems, to Ingeborg Glier for casting light on what seemed to me some impenetrable lines of Middle High German, and to Laurel Fay for help in the English version of Musorgsky's song.

A number of research assistants, all former students at Yale, shared in the background research, in many of the routine tasks, and in some of the joys of discovery and critical selection while the first edition of this anthology was being prepared. Robert Ford and Carolyn Abbate explored options in pre-Baroque and post-Classical music respectively. Gail Hilson Woldu and Kenneth Suzuki surveyed the literature on a sizable number of the items, while Susan Cox Carlson contributed her expertise in early polyphony. Clara Marvin assisted in manifold ways in the last stages of the first edition.

My colleagues at Yale and elsewhere were generous with their advice on selections, particularly Margot Fassler on the Mass, my wife Elizabeth Keitel on Machaut, Craig Wright on Dufay, Leon Plantinga on Clementi, Gayle Sherwood on Ives, Allen Forte on Schoenberg, and Laurel Fay on Shostakovich and Gubaidulina.

The Yale Music Library was my indispensable base of operations, and its staff a prime resource for the development of this anthology. I wish to thank particularly Harold Samuel, Music Librarian Emeritus, his successor Kendall Crilly, and their associates Kathryn R. Mansi and Helen Bartlett. Karl W. Schrom, record librarian, was a remarkable fount of knowledge and advice about recorded performances.

John J. H. Muller as adviser to the publisher on the recorded anthology contributed to this edition of the CDs and cassettes through his excellent suggestions and quality control.

This anthology owes very much to Claire Brook, who, as the former music editor of Norton, proposed the idea of an anthology to accompany the third edition of Donald J. Grout's *A History of Western Music*. She has continued to assist in the production of this third edition of the anthology. I also benefited from the advice of Norton's present music editor, Michael Ochs, in adjusting the content to the changing needs of the field. Thanks as well to Gabrielle Karp, for capably guiding the two volumes through the production process.

W. W. Norton and I are grateful to the individuals and publishers cited in the source notes who granted permission to reprint, re-edit, or adapt material under copyright. Where no modern publication is cited, the music was edited from original sources.

CLAUDE V. PALISCA
Hamden, Connecticut

RECORDINGS

Recordings accompanying this anthology are available under the titles *Norton Recorded Anthology of Western Music* (12 CDs or cassettes, containing all the pieces in the two volumes) and *Concise Norton Recorded Anthology of Western Music* (4 CDs or cassettes, containing 69 of the pieces in the two volumes). Track numbers for both sets of CDs are indicated in the scores as follows:

12-CD set (tracks indicated by boxed numbers):

CD 1: NAWM 1–22   **CD 7:** NAWM 87–99
CD 2: NAWM 23–43   **CD 8:** NAWM 100–107
CD 3: NAWM 44–56   **CD 9:** NAWM 108–120
CD 4: NAWM 57–70   **CD 10:** NAWM 121–127
CD 5: NAWM 71–82   **CD 11:** NAWM 128–140
CD 6: NAWM 83–86   **CD 12:** NAWM 141–152

4-CD set (tracks indicated by diamond-shaped boxes):

CD 1: NAWM 1–46   **CD 3:** NAWM 87–122
CD 2: NAWM 47–85   **CD 4:** NAWM 124–151

NORTON ANTHOLOGY OF *Western Music*

THIRD EDITION

VOLUME *1*

Ancient to Baroque

Epitaph of Seikilos

1.

Musical notes

C Z̄ Ž̄ κ ι Z ι̇̄

῞Οσον ζῆς φαί — νου

Text rhythm   S L   L   L   L
Musical rhythm   S L L+S S S S L+S

2.

Musical notes

K̄ ι Ż ι̱̇ K O C̄ O̱ φ̄

μηδὲν ὅλ—ως σὺ λυ–ποῦ·

Text rhythm   L S S L D D L
Musical rhythm   L S S SS S L S+L

3.

Musical notes

C K Z ι̇ ḱ ι K C̄ O̱ φ̄

πρὸς ὀλίγον ἐ—στὶ τὸ ζῆν,

Text rhythm   S S D S L   D S   L
Musical rhythm   S S S S SS S L S+L

4.

Musical notes

C K O ι Ż ḱ C C̄   C X̄⌐

τὸ τέλος ὁ χρόνος ἀπαι–τεῖ.

Text rhythm   S S S C S S D L   L
Musical rhythm   S S S S S S S L   S+L

D = dichronic syllable
S = short syllable
L = long syllable
C = common syllable

As long as you live, be lighthearted.
Let nothing trouble you.
Life is only too short,
and time takes its toll.

Copenhagen, National Museum, Inventory No. 14897 (for photograph, see HWM, p. 15). Analytical transcription by Thomas J. Mathiesen in "Rhythm and Meter in Ancient Greek Music," *Music Theory Spectrum* 7 (1985):171–72. Used by permission.

The Seikilos epitaph is inscribed on a tomb stele, or tombstone, found in Aidin, Turkey, near Tralles and dating from around the first century A.D. (Copenhagen, Inventory Number 14897; see illustration in HWM, p. 15). Lines of text are accompanied by letters representing pitches in the Greek notation and by signs indicating their duration. It is a *skolion*, or drinking song, attributed in the first lines to Seikilos.

It is possible to analyze the tonal structure of this brief song in terms of the criteria developed by the theorists of the time.

Every note of the octave *e–e'*, with *F* and *C* sharped, is in the song, so that the octave species is unambiguously identifiable as that called Phrygian by Cleonides, equivalent to the *D*-octave on the white keys of a piano. The most prominent notes are *a* and the two boundary notes *e* and *e'*. The note *a* is the most frequent note (eight occurrences), and three of the four phrases begin on it; *e'* is the topmost pitch in all four phrases and occurs six times; *e* is the final note of the piece. Of subsidiary importance are *g*, which closes two of the phrases but is skipped over at the end, and *d'*, which closes one.

The prominence of *a* is significant, because it is the central note or mese of the Greater Perfect System. In the *Problems* attributed to Aristotle that may include writings of others, it is stated: "In all good music *mese* occurs frequently, and all good composers have frequent recourse to *mese*, and, if they leave it, they soon return to it, as they do to no other note."[*]

The *e–e'* octave with two sharps is a segment of the two-octave scale *B–b'* with two sharps, identified by Alypius as the diatonic Iastian tonos, a lower form of the Phrygian that is also known as Ionian (see analysis of the inscription on facing page). This tonos transposes the Greater Perfect System up a whole tone from its natural, Hypolydian, location *A–a'* in the notation of Alypius. The identity of the tonos seems almost incidental to the structure of the piece, however, because the pitches that are most prominent, *a* and *e'*, function as lichanos meson and paranete diezeugmenon in that tonos, both non-stable steps (see HWM, p. 10, Example 1.3). In the thetic scale, on the other hand, the notes *e*, *a*, and *e'* are hypate meson, mese, and nete diezeugmenon, all stable notes, and the species of fifth *a–e'*, which dominates most of the piece, and the species of fourth *e–a* that prevails at the end, divide the species of octave into two consonant halves.

So far as the ethos of the song is concerned, it seems to be neither excited nor depressed, but balanced between the two extremes, which is consistent with the Ionian tonos. In terms of Alypius' arrangement of the fifteen tonoi, the Ionian, with proslambanomenos on *B* and mese on *b*, is intermediate between the lowest, Hypodorian, with proslambanomenos on *F* and mese on *f*, and the highest, Hyperlydian, with proslambanomenos on *g* and mese on *g'*. The major thirds would be perceived today, and probably then

---

[*]Aristotle, *Problems* 19.20 (919a), trans. E. M. Forster in *The Works of Aristotle,* ed. W. D. Ross, vol. 7, *Problemata* (Oxford: Clarendon Press, 1927).

also, as bright, as would the rising fifth of the opening. The message of the poem is, indeed, optimistic.

The Seikilos song has been of particular interest to historians because of its clear rhythmic notation. The notes without rhythmic markings above the alphabetical signs are worth a unit of duration (*chronos protos*); the horizontal dash indicates a *diseme*, worth two beats, and the horizontal mark with an upward stroke to the right is a *triseme* worth three. Each line has twelve beats.

Analysis of Seikilos Inscription

Thetic names		*Name by function* (Iastian tonos)	*Species* (Phrygian)
fixed nete diezeugmenon	e′	paranete diezeugmenon	
			Tone
paranete diezeugm.	d	trite diezeugmenon	
			Semitone
trite diezeugmenon	c♯	paramese	
		disjunction	Tone
fixed paramese	b	mese	
disjunction			Tone
fixed mese	a	lichanos meson	
			Tone
lichanos meson	g	parhypate meson	
			Tone
parhypate meson	f♯	hypate meson	
			Semitone
fixed hypate meson	e	lichanos hypaton	
			Tone

2 EURIPIDES (CA. 485–CA. 406 B.C.)

Orestes: Stasimon Chorus

Fragment, lines 338–44

1.

Musical notes   π̄   P C   Ṗ φ π

κατολοφ]ύ - ρομαι ί ματέρος [αἷμα σᾶς

Text rhythm   D S S D   S L | D S S   L D D

Musical rhythm   L   S L | S S S

2.

Musical notes   (?)–   i Z E

ὅ σ' ἀναβα]κχεύει ἱ ὁ μέγας [ὄλβος οὐ

Text rhythm   S   D D L   L L | S S D   L S L

Musical rhythm   L   L L | S S S

3.

Musical notes   π̄   P C   i Z

μόνιμο]ς ἐμ βροτοῖς ἱ ἀνὰ [δὲ λαῖφος ὥς

Text rhythm   S D S   L(S?)S L | D D   S L S L

Musical rhythm   L   S L | S S

4.

Musical notes   C P π̄   C P   i φ C–

τι]ς ἀκάτου θοᾶς τινά[ξας δαίμων

Text rhythm   D   D D L   S L | D L L   L L

Musical rhythm   S S L   S L | S L

D = dichronic syllable | = possible position of the thesis

S = short syllable   C = common syllable

L = long syllable

Vienna, Österreichische Nationalbibliothek, Papyrus G2315. Analytical transcription by Thomas J. Mathiesen in "Rhythm and Meter in Ancient Greek Music," *Music Theory Spectrum* 7 (1985):177. Used by permission.

5.

Musical notes

Text rhythm   D   C   D   S   L   L

Musical rhythm   S   S   S   L   ⊻   S S

6.

Musical notes

Text rhythm   S   L   L   L   L

Musical rhythm   ⊻ S S   SS   L

7.   Musical notes

[text uncertain]

You wild goddesses who dart across the skies seeking vengeance for murder, we implore you to free Agamemnon's son from his raging fury. . . . We grieve for this boy. Happiness is brief among mortals. Sorrow and anguish sweep down on it like a swift gust of wind on a sloop, and it sinks under the tossing seas.

This fragment of the chorus from Euripides' *Orestes* is on a papyrus from the third to the second century B.C. The tragedy has been dated 408 B.C. It is possible that the music was composed by Euripides himself, who was renowned for his musical settings. This chorus is a *stasimon*, an ode sung while the chorus stood still in its place in the *orchestra*, a semicircular rim between the stage and the benches of the spectators.

The papyrus contains seven lines with musical notation, but only the middle of each of the seven lines survives; the beginning and end of each line of text are shown within brackets. Forty-two notes of the piece survive, but because a good many are missing, any performance must be a reconstruction, like that in the recording that accompanies this anthology.

Some of the alphabetical signs are vocal and some instrumental; some are enharmonic (or chromatic) and some diatonic (see the analysis on the following page). This transcription renders the dense intervals as chromatic, but by varying the "shade," these could be converted to the denser enharmonic. The surviving notes fit into the Lydian tonos of Alypius. The three lowest notes of the diezeugmenon tetrachord are separated by the tone of disjunction from the chromatic meson tetrachord, which in turn is conjoined with the diatonic hypaton tetrachord, whose top two notes are used. The piece, therefore, seems to be written in a mixture of the chromatic and diatonic genera. The octave species, or *harmonia*, appears to be Phrygian, but two harmoniae described as dating from the time of Plato by the musical theorist and philosopher Aristides Quintilianus (fourth century A.D.)—his Dorian and Phrygian—almost exactly coincide with the scale that is found here, as the analysis of the *Orestes* Stasimon fragment below shows.

Analysis of *Orestes* Stasimon Fragment

Dynamic names	Phryg. diat.	octave spec.	Alypius signs for Lydian enharmonic voc.	inst.	Aristides Q. harmoniae Dorian	Phrygian
					a′ ⊖	
						g′ Ⴑ
paranete diezeugmenon	g′	T		Z	f′ △	f′ △
trite diezeugmenon	f′	S	E		e′ + E	e′ + E
paramese	e′		Z		e′ Z	e′ Z
(disjunction)		T				
mese	d′				d′ I	d′ I
lichanos meson chrom.	b	T	Π	Ɔ	a♯ Π	a♯ Π
parhypate meson	b♭	T	Ρ		a + Ρ	a + Ρ
hypate meson	a	S	C		a C	a C
lichanos hypaton	g	T	φ		g φ	g φ
[parhypate hypaton]	[f]					
hypate hypaton	e			٦		

In the stasimon, the women of Argos implore the gods to have mercy on Orestes, who had murdered his mother, Clytemnestra, six days before the play begins. He had plotted with his sister Electra to punish their mother for infidelity to their father, Agamemnon. The chorus begs that Orestes be released from the madness that has overwhelmed him since the murder. The rhythm of the poetry, and therefore of the music, is dominated by the dochmiac foot, which was used in Greek tragedy during passages of intense agitation and grief. The dochmiac consists of three long followed by two short syllables, but often, as here, a long syllable is resolved into two short ones, so that instead of five notes per foot there are six. In the transcription, the feet are separated by vertical bars in the "text rhythm" symbols.

The singing of the text is interrupted by instrumental sounds, *g′* in lines 1 through 4, *e′–b* in lines 5 and 6. The hypate hypaton (*a*) is prominent, in that two of the lines of verse (punctuated in lines 1 and 3 by the instrumental note *g*) end on that note, and a number of phrases of the melody are clustered around the paramese *e′*; both *a* and *e* are stable pitches in the Lydian tonos, and they are the lowest steps in the two tetrachords utilized in the piece (see the analysis above).*

*A rhythmic analysis of this fragment is in Thomas J. Mathiesen, "Rhythm and Meter in Ancient Greek Music," *Music Theory Spectrum* 7 (1985):159–80. Used by permission.

GREGORIAN CHANT

Mass for Christmas Day

3

Instructions for Reading Modern Plainchant Notation

One line of the four-line staff is designated by a clef as either middle *C* (𝄡) or the *F* immediately below it (𝄢). These are not absolute but relative pitches. The *neumes*, as the shapes are called, are usually assigned equal durations, although at one time they may have had some temporal significance. Two or more neumes in succession on the same line or space, if on the same syllable, are sung as though tied. Composite neumes, representing two or more pitches, are read from left to right, except for the *podatus* or *pes* (𝅘𝅥), in which the lower note is sung first. Oblique neumes (◥) stand for two different pitches. A neume, whether simple or composite, never carries more than one syllable. Flat signs, except in a signature at the beginning of a line, are valid only until the next vertical division line or until the beginning of the next word.

The Vatican editions, such as the *Liber usualis* (*LU*), employ in addition a number of interpretive signs, based on the performance practices of the Benedictine monks of the Solesmes Congregation. A horizontal dash above or below a neume means it is to be slightly lengthened. A vertical stroke above or below a note marks the beginning of a rhythmic unit when this would not otherwise be obvious. A dot after a note doubles its value. Vertical bars of varied lengths show the division of a melody into periods (full bar), phrases (half-bar), and smaller members (a stroke through the uppermost staff-line). The note-like symbol on a space or line at the end of the staff is a *custos* (guard), a guide to lead the reader to the first note on the following line.

An asterisk in the text shows where the chorus takes over from the soloist, and the signs *ij* and *iij* (ditto and double-ditto) indicate that the preceding phrase is to be sung twice or three times.

The music for each of the major feasts of the church calendar has special qualities, and that is true of the Mass for Christmas Day (*in die Natali*). The Proper chants are unique to this day in the church calendar. A variety of Ordinary chants may be used, but they must include the Gloria, which is omitted during certain times in the liturgical year. Beginning in the thirteenth century, Ordinary chants were organized into *cycles*; the Ordinary chants chosen for this anthology are taken from a Mass cycle whose Kyrie-Gloria pair occurs in manuscripts as early as the twelfth century and is numbered V in the *Liber usualis* (pp. 28–31). Neither the chants of the Proper of a given day nor the Ordinary cycle shows any consistency of age or mode. The neumes on the four-line staff indicate relative pitch; the cantor chose a pitch that suited the singers' voices.

a) Introit: *Puer natus est nobis*

Puer natus est nobis, et filius datus est nobis:
cujus imperium super humerum ejus:
et vocabitur nomen ejus, magni consili
Angelus.
Ps. Cantate Domino canticum novum: quia
mirabilia fecit.
℣. Gloria Patri, et Filio, et Spiritui Sancto. Sicut
erat in principio, et nunc, et semper, et in
saecula saeculorum.
Amen.

A child is born to us, and a Son is given to us;
whose government is upon His shoulder;
and His Name shall be called the Angel of great
counsel.
Ps. Sing ye to the Lord a new canticle, because He
hath done wonderful things.
℣. Glory be to the Father, and to the Son, and to
the Holy Ghost. As it was in the beginning, is
now, and ever shall be, world without end.
Amen.

The sung portion of the Mass begins with the Introit. The Introit *Puer natus est nobis* was often troped (received added words and music) as a dramatic dialogue (see NAWM 7). Two chant styles may be distinguished in this and

Ordinaries from Mass V, *Liber usualis*, pp. 28–31. Propers from *LU*, 408–410.

other Introits. One style is used to sing the psalm verse (indicated by *Ps.*) and the Gloria Patri, or Lesser Doxology (praise to God), which follows the psalm verse (concerning the Doxology, see below, p. 12). In this recitational manner the melody holds mostly to one pitch—here *D*, the reciting tone of Mode 7, the mode of this Introit—with opening rises and cadential falls, one or two notes per syllable. The other style, more varied and florid, is that of the antiphon—the music preceding the psalm (and normally sung again after the psalm verse). Both the antiphon and the psalm verse end on *G*, the final of Modes 7 and 8. The antiphon shows traces of the reciting tone *C*, which is used in several modes but not in the seventh mode. Like this Introit, many return frequently to the note *C*, even if it is not the reciting tone of the mode.

b) Kyrie

Kyrie eleison. Christe eleison.   Lord have mercy. Christ have mercy.
Kyrie eleison.   Lord have mercy.

After the Introit the choir chants the Kyrie. Among the musical settings of the Kyrie that may be sung on this Sunday is one known as *Kyrie magnae Deus potentiae*, from the thirteenth century. The invocation "Kyrie eleison" (Lord have mercy) is repeated three times; then "Christe eleison" (Christ have mercy) is repeated three times, after which the threefold Kyrie is sung again. The simplest settings use one melody for all the Kyries and a different melody for all the Christes, and that is the pattern followed here.

This chant is classified as being in Mode 8. It fits the plagal range by extending upward a fifth from the final *g* and downward it exceeds the range by a second to *c*.

c) Gloria

8.

G Ló-ri- a in excélsis Dé- o. Et in térra pax ho-

mí-ni-bus bónae vo-luntá-tis. Laudámus te.   Bene-dí-ci-

mus te. Adorámus te. Glo-ri- fi-cámus te. Grá- ti- as

á-gimus tí- bi   propter mágnam gló-   ri- am tú- am.

Dó- mi-ne Dé- us   Rex caeléstis, Dé-us Pá-ter   o- mní-

pot-ens. Dó- mi-ne   Fí-li unigéni-te   Jé-su Chríste.

Dómine Dé- us   A- gnus Dé- i,   Fí- li- us Pá- tris. Qui

tól-lis peccáta múndi,   mi-se- ré-   re nó-bis. Qui tól-

lis   peccá-ta múndi,   súscipe depre-ca-ti-   ónem nóstram. Qui sé-des ad déxteram Pátris, mi-se- ré-

re nó-bis. Quó- ni- am tu só-lus sánctus. Tu só- lus Dó-

minus. Tu só- lus Al- tíssimus, Jé- su Chrí- ste. Cum

Sáncto Spí-ri-tu, in gló-ri- a Dé- i Pá- tris. A-

men.

Gloria in excelsis Deo	Glory be to God on high.
Et in terra pax hominibus bonae voluntatis.	And on earth peace to men of good will.
Laudamus te. Benedicimus te. Adoramus te. Glorificamus te.	We praise thee, we bless thee, we adore thee, we glorify thee.
Gratias agimus tibi propter magnam gloriam tuam.	We give thee thanks for thy great glory.
Domine Deus, Rex caelestis,	O Lord God, King of heaven,
Deus Pater omnipotens.	God the Father Almighty.
Domine Fili unigenite Jesu Christe.	O Lord, the only begotten Son, Jesus Christ.
Domine Deus, Agnus Dei, Filius Patris.	O Lord God, Lamb of God, Son of the Father.
Qui tollis peccata mundi, miserere nobis.	Thou who takest away the sins of the world, have mercy on us.
Qui tollis peccata mundi, suscipe deprecationem nostram.	Thou who takest away the sins of the world, receive our prayer.
Qui sedes ad dexteram Patris, miserere nobis.	Thou who sittest at the right hand of the Father, have mercy on us.
Quoniam tu solus sanctus.	For thou only art holy,
Tu solus Dominus.	Thou only art Lord.
Tu solus Altissimus, Jesu Christe.	Thou only art most high, O Jesus Christ,
Cum Sancto Spiritu,	With the Holy Ghost,
In Gloria Dei Patris. Amen.	In the glory of God the Father. Amen.

Because the Gloria, or Greater Doxology, has a relatively long text, most syllables are sung to only one, two, or three notes. This chant, in the eighth mode, holds strictly to its plagal octave between *d* and *d′*. The *Liber usualis* attributes it to the twelfth century, and it shows its late date by its unusual pattern of melodic repetition. The melodic units repeated are sometimes shorter, sometimes longer than a textual phrase. For example, the melody for "in excelsis Deo" is set to the complete sentence "Benedicimus te," the unpunctuated phrase "agimus tibi," and eight other segments of text. The melodic member first heard at "Laudamus te" serves three other two-word groups, four single words, and the syllable "A" of "A-men." The longest melodic element, first heard at "Et in terra pax hominibus," is split between two sentences at "Adoramus te. Glorificamus te," with the melisma broken up into four syllables. The melody is heard six more times, with the melisma kept intact. The reciting tone *c′*, usually prominent in a wordy text, plays no part in the composition.

After the Gloria a prayer called the Collect is chanted to a very simple formula, practically a monotone. Then the Epistle, one of the letters of the apostle Paul to the Hebrews, is recited, again to a simple formula.

d) Gradual: *Viderunt omnes*

ve-lá-   vit * justí-   ti- am sú- am.

Viderunt omnes fines terrae salutare Dei nostri: jubilate Deo omnis terra. ℣. Notum fecit Dominus salutare suum: ante conspectum gentium revelavit justitiam suam.	All the ends of the earth have seen the salvation of our God; sing joyfully to God, all the earth. ℣. The Lord hath made known His salvation; He hath revealed His justice in the sight of the Gentiles.

This Gradual exemplifies responsorial psalmody, in which a soloist singing the psalm (Vulgate Ps. 97 [Eng. 98]:3-4, 2) alternates with a choir performing the respond. The extended melismas of *omnes* and *terrae*—typical of Graduals—received polyphonic elaboration in the twelfth century. Unlike the Introit's psalm verse, which was recitational, this verse is extremely ornate, intended as it was for a soloist, although the recitation tone *C* is prominent. Many Graduals exhibit a structure unified by motivic repetition, but this example does not. The fifth mode is frequently used in Graduals, as it is here. Its final is *F*, and the note *B* is sometimes flatted to avoid the melodic tritone.

e) Alleluia

2.

Lle-lú-ia. * *ij.*   ℣. Dí-

es sancti-ficátus illúxit nó-   bis :

ve-   ní-te géntes, et adorá-te Dómi-

num : qui-a hó-di-   e   descéndit lux má-

gna * su-per tér- ram.

Alleluia. Alleluia.

℣. Dies sanctificatus illuxit nobis: venite gentes, et adorate Dominum: quia hodie descendit lux magna super terram.

Alleluia, alleluia.

℣. A sanctified day hath shone upon us; come ye Gentiles, and adore the Lord; for this day a great light hath descended upon the earth.

During most of the year, the Alleluia, another responsorial chant, follows the Gradual. As in the Gradual, a soloist sang the psalm verse, while the choir responded with "Alleluia"—from the Hebrew "Hallelujah" (praise Yahweh, or Jehovah). The Alleluia for Christmas Day is one of the oldest; it lacks the extended melisma on the final "a" called the *jubilus*. The phrases of this chant end mainly on the final of the second mode, *D*; some of them end on *C* and one on *A*, but none closes on the reciting tone *F*.

After the Alleluia comes the reading of the Gospel, which is chanted on a simple recitation formula. The priest then intones "Credo in unum Deum" (I believe in one God), and the choir continues from "Patrem omnipotentem" (the Father Almighty) to the end of the Nicene Creed. Credo melodies were not included in the Ordinary cycles, and this chant is omitted also from this anthology for economy of space. (For the text and a translation of the Credo, see NAWM 49.) The Credo, together with the sermon (if any), marks the end of the first main division of the Mass, to be followed by the Eucharist proper.

f) Offertory: *Tui sunt caeli*

ti- a et judí- ci- um praepa-rá-

ti-o sé- dis tú- ae.

Tui sunt caeli, et tua est terra:
  orbem terrarum, et plenitudinem ejus tu
  fundasti: justitia et judicium
  praeparatio sedis tuae.

Thine are the heavens, and Thine is the earth:
  the world and the fullness thereof Thou
  hast founded; justice and judgment
  are the preparation of Thy throne.

As the preparation of the bread and wine begins, the Offertory is sung, during which donations to the church are offered. In earlier times this was an occasion for the singing of Psalms; all that survives today is a verse or two, as in the Offertory *Tui sunt caeli*. This Offertory uses verse 11 and half of verse 13 from the Vulgate Ps. 88 (English 89). But the music is not in psalmodic style, and there is no trace of the fourth mode's reciting tone *A*, a note rarely reached in this low-placed plagal melody. Rather, the music is graced by exuberant melismas.

The priest now says various prayers in a speaking voice for the blessing of the elements and vessels of the Eucharist, the reenactment of Christ's last supper. One prayer that is chanted is the Preface, to a formula that is more melodious than the other simple readings.

g) Sanctus

SAn- ctus, * Sán-ctus, Sán- ctus Dóminus Dé-us Sá- ba- oth. Pléni sunt caéli et térra gló-ri- a tú- a.

Ho- sánna in excél- sis. Benedíctus qui vé-nit in

nómi-ne Dómi-ni. Ho- sánna in excél- sis.

Sanctus, Sanctus, Sanctus Dominus Deus Sabaoth.
  Pleni sunt caeli et terra gloria tua.
  Hosanna in excelsis. Benedictus qui venit
  in nomine Domini. Hosanna in excelsis.

Holy, holy, holy, Lord God of Hosts.
  The heavens and earth are full of thy glory.
  Hosanna in the highest. Blessed is he who comes
  in the name of the Lord. Hosanna in the highest.

The Sanctus ("Holy, holy, holy") and Benedictus ("Blessed is he who comes") are both sung by the choir. In Mass V, a twelfth-century chant, the composer took advantage of the threefold "Sanctus" and the twofold "Hosanna" to achieve a symmetrical form at the beginning and end. The melody, in the fourth mode, rises a sixth above the final *e* but only a second below. It hovers around the reciting tone *a*.

Now the celebrant pronounces the Canon, the prayer consecrating the bread and wine, and the congregation recites the prayer *Pater noster* (the Lord's Prayer, "Our Father, who art in heaven . . .").

h) Agnus Dei

A- gnus Dé- i, * qui tól- lis pec-cá- ta mún-

di : mi-seré- re nó- bis. A- gnus Dé- i, * qui tól-

lis pec-cá- ta mún-di : mi-se-ré- re nó- bis. Agnus Dé- i, * qui tól- lis pec- cá- ta mún-di : dóna

nó- bis pá- cem.

Agnus Dei, qui tollis peccata
   mundi: miserere nobis. Agnus Dei,
   qui tollis peccata mundi: miserere
   nobis. Agnus Dei, qui tollis peccata
   mundi: dona nobis pacem.

Lamb of God, who takest away the sins
   of the world, have mercy on us. Lamb of God,
   who takest away the sins of the world, have mercy
   on us. Lamb of God, who takest away the sins
   of the world: give us peace.

The cantor and choir sing the Agnus Dei. The text consists of a threefold
acclamation, "Lamb of God, who takest away the sins of the world," followed by two identical responses, "have mercy on us," and a final response,
"give us peace." Despite the two different responses, the three Agnus periods
have the same music. Moreover, the responses echo the music of "qui tollis
peccata."

i) Communion: *Viderunt omnes*

Idé- runt ómnes * fí-nes tér- rae   sa-lu-

tá- re Dé- i nóstri.

Viderunt omnes fines terrae salutare
   Dei nostri.

All the ends of the earth have seen the salvation
   of our God.

After the faithful and celebrants have partaken of the bread and wine, the
choir sings the Communion. Originally an antiphon-psalm pair sung during
the distribution of the bread and wine, the psalm was dropped by the
twelfth century and only the antiphon remained. The text of this unusually

short Communion is the same as that beginning the Gradual. The pattern of cadences in the first mode suggests a deliberate search for variety: *D, E, F,* and *D.*

j) Ite, missa est

8.

- te,
Dé-o

míssa est.
grá- ti- as.

Ite, missa est.
Deo gratia.

Go, the Mass is over.
Thanks to God.

This short chant returns to the eighth mode of the Kyrie. The statements are set strophically, with a lengthy melisma on the first word followed by a syllabic cadence. (The "Ite, missa est" is not sung in the recording.)

GREGORIAN CHANT

Office of Second Vespers, *Nativity of Our Lord*

Although considerably more ornate than most, the Second Vespers of the feast of the Nativity of Our Lord (December 25) is typical of the Office celebrated at sunset. The service begins with introductory prayers, including the *Pater noster* (the Lord's Prayer) and the *Ave Maria* (Hail Mary).

(The recordings accompanying this anthology contain a sample Antiphon, *Tecum principium*, Psalm 109, *Dixit Dominus*, and the Short Responsory and Verse, *Notum fecit*. The remaining antiphons and psalms are omitted from the record set for reasons of economy.)

a) Verse: *Deus in adjutorium*

V. Deus, in adjutorium meum intende.
R. Domine, ad adiuvandum me festina.
Gloria Patri, et Filio, et Spiritui Sancto. Sicut erat in principio, et nunc, et semper, et in saecula saeculorum. Amen. Alleluia.

V. O God, come to my assistance.
R. O Lord, make haste to help me.
Glory be to the Father, and to the Son, and to the Holy Ghost. As it was in the beginning, is now and ever shall be, world without end. Amen. Alleluia.

The first verse of Psalm 69, *Deus in adjutorium,* is sung to a special formula somewhat more elaborate than the usual psalm tone.

English translations from *The Saint Andrew Daily Missal,* ed. Dom Gaspar Lefebvre, O.S.B. (New York: Benziger Press, 1956). Reprinted by permission. The Chapter, Kyrie, *Pater noster,* and Prayer (*Oratio*) have been omitted. Antiphons, Short Responsory and Verse *Notum fecit* from *Antiphonale monasticum,* pp. 245–49. *Deus in adjutorium: Liber usualis (LU),* p. 112; Psalm 109: *LU,* p. 128, Tone 1g; Psalm 110: *LU,* p. 139, Tone 7a; Psalm 111: *LU,* p. 146, Tone 7d; Psalm 129: *LU,* p. 178, Tone 4A; Magnificat: *LU,* p. 213, Tone 1g[2].

b) Antiphon: *Tecum principium*

ECUM prin-cí- pi- um * in di- e virtú-tis

tu- æ, in splendó-ri-bus sanctó-rum, ex ú-te-ro ante lu-cí-

fe-rum gé-nu- i te.   E u o u a e.

Tecum principium in die
   virtutis tuae in splendoribus
   sanctorum, ex utero ante luciferum
   genui te.

Thine shall be the dominion in the day
   of Thy strength in the brightness
   of the Saints, from the womb before the day star
   I begot Thee.

c) Psalm 109: *Dixit Dominus*

Mediant of 2 accents.

1. Dí-xit Dóminus Dómino mé- o ; * Séde a *déxtris* mé- is.

1 Díxit Dóminus **Dó**mino **mé**o: *
    Séde a *déxtris* **mé**is.
2 Donec pónam ini**mí**cos **tú**os, *
    scabéllum pé*dum tu*órum.
3 Vírgam virtútis túae emíttet Dómi**nus**
    ex **Sí**on: * dománáre in médio
    inimicó*rum tu*órum.
4 Técum princípium in díe virtútis túae
    in splendóri**bus** sanctó**rum**: *
    ex útero ante lucíferum
    *génu*i te.

The Lord said unto my Lord:
   Sit Thou at My right hand.
Until I make Thine enemies
   Thy footstool.
The Lord shall send the rod of Thy strength
   out of Sion: rule Thou in the midst
   of Thine enemies.
Thine shall be the dominion in the day
   of Thy strength amid the brightness of the
   Saints: from the womb, before the day star
   have I begotten Thee.

5 Jurávit Dóminus, et non paeni**té**bit **é**um: ★
  Tu es sacérdos in aetérnum secúndum **órdi***nem*
  *Mel***chi**sedech.

6 Dóminus a **déx**tris **tú**is, ★
  confrégit in díe írae *súae* **ré**ges.

7 Judicábit in natiónibus,
  im**plé**bit ru**í**nas: ★
  conquassábit cápita in tér*ra mul***tó**rum.

8 De torrénte in **ví**a **bí**bet: ★
  proptérea exal*tábit* **cá**put.

9 Glória **Pá**tri, et **Fí**lio, ★
  et Spirí*tui* **Sán**cto.

10 Sicut érat in princípio, et **núnc,**
   et **sém**per, ★ et in saécula saecu*lórum.*
   Amen.

The Lord hath sworn, and will not repent:
  Thou art a Priest for ever after the order of
  Melchisedech.

The Lord at Thy right hand shall strike
  through kings in the day of His wrath.

He shall judge among the heathen,
  He shall fill the places with dead bodies:
  He shall wound the heads over many countries.

He shall drink of the brook in the way
  therefore shall He lift up His head.

Glory be to the Father, and to the Son,
  and to the Holy Ghost.

As it was in the beginning, is now,
  and ever shall be, world without end.
  Amen.

The first full psalm sung in this Office is Psalm 109, *Dixit Dominus.* It is preceded by the Antiphon *Tecum principium.* Since this antiphon is in the first
mode, the psalm tone for this mode is chosen, but provided with an ending
on *G* rather than the final *D,* so that it may lead back easily into the first
notes, *E–C,* of the antiphon. This alternate ending is called a *differentia* (difference). The conclusion of the antiphon brings the melody around to the
final *D.* After the last verse of the psalm, the Lesser Doxology (from the
Greek *doxologia,* a praising), beginning with the words *Gloria Patri* and ending with *saeculorum. Amen,* is sung to the same formula. This Doxology formula is often abbreviated "Euouae," standing for the sound of the vowels in
sAEcUlOrUm. AmEn.

d) Antiphon: *Redemptionem misit Dominus*

dávit in æ·tér·num   testamén·tum su· um. E u o u a e.

Redemptionem misit Dominus populo suo,
  mandavit in aeternum testamentum suum.

The Lord hath sent redemption to His people,
  He hath commanded his convenant for ever.

e) Psalm 110: *Confitebor tibi Domine*

† This symbol in a psalm text calls for a Flex.

* This symbol in a psalm text marks the closing versicle, which is sung to the Tenor followed by the Termination

◌ The hollow note is sung when there are two unaccented syllables after the accented one, as in *ó-pe-ra Dó-mi-ni.*

1 Confitebor tibi, Domine, in toto corde meo:
in consilio iustorum,
et congregatione.

2 Magna opera Domini: exquisita
in omnes voluntates eius.

3 Confesso et magnificentia opus eius:
et iustitia eius manet in saeculum saeculi.

4 Memoriam fecit mirabilium suorum,
misericors et miserator Dominus:
escam dedit
timentibus se.

5 Memor erit in saeculum testamenti
sui: virtutem operum suorum
annuntiabit populo suo:

I will praise Thee, O Lord, with my whole heart:
in the assembly of the upright,
and in the congregation.

The works of the Lord are great, meet
to serve for the doing of His will.

His work is honorable and glorious,
and His righteousness endureth for ever.

He hath made a memorial of his wonderful
works: the Lord is gracious and full of
compassion. He hath given meat unto
them that fear Him:

He will ever be mindful of His convenant.
He will show His people the power
of His works:

Tenor   Termination of 2 accents

1 *in con-si - li - o ju-sto-rum, et con-gre -   ga -   ti - o -   ne.
2 *ex - qui-si - ta in om-nes vo-lun-   ta -   tes e -   jus.
3 *et jus-ti - ti - a   e-jus ma-net in   sae - cu-lum sae - cu - li.

4 * es - cam de - dit ti -   men -   ti - bus   se.
5 *vir - tu-tem o - pe-rum su - o-rum an -nun-ci - a- bit po- pu - lo su   o.
6 * o - pe - ra ma-nu-um   e-jus ve - ri- tas   et   ju - di - ci - um.

7 * fac - ta in   ve - ri - ta - te et   ae -   qui - ta -   te.
8 *man - da-vit in ae - ter-num te - sta -   men - tum su -   um.
9 * i - ni - ti - um sa - pi - en - ti - ae   ti -   mor Do - mi - ni.
10 * lau - da - tio   e-jus ma-net in   sae - cu-lum sae - cu - li.
11 * et Spi-ri -   tu -   i San   cto.
12 * et   in sae - cu-la sae-cu -   lo -   rum. A -   men.

6 Ut det illis haereditatem gentium:
   opera manuum eius veritas et iudicium.
7 Fidelia omnia mandata eius:
   confirmata in saeculum saeculi:
   facta in veritate et aequitate.
8 Redemptionem misit populo suo:
   mandavit in aeternum testamentum suum.
9 Sanctum et terribile nomen eius:
   initium sapientiae timor Domini.
10 Intellectus bonus omnibus
   facientibus eum: laudatio eius manet in
   saeculum saeculi.
11 Gloria Patri, et Filio,
   et Spiritui Sancto.
12 Sicut erat in principio, et nunc,
   et semper, et in saecula saeculorum.
   Amen.

That He may give them the heritage of the heathen.
   The works of His hands are verity and judgment:
All His commandments are sure:
   they stand fast for ever and ever,
   being done in truth and uprightness.
He sent redemption unto His people:
   He hath commanded His convenant for ever:
Holy and terrible is His name.
   The fear of the Lord is the beginning of wisdom.
A good understanding have all they that
   do His commandments: His praise endureth
   for ever.
Glory be to the Father, and to the Son,
   and to the Holy Ghost.
As it was in the beginning, is now,
   and ever shall be, world without end.
   Amen.

Return to Antiphon, *Redemptionem*

Selection e shows how the psalm-tone formula is applied to the singing of a psalm. (See HWM, p. 45, Example 2.3: Outline of the Psalmody of the Office.) There is one tone or formula for each of the eight church modes and an extra one called the *Tonus peregrinus,* or "wandering tone." The formula for the first half of the verse has three components: the *initium,* or intonation (used only in the first verse of the psalm), the reciting tone, or *tenor,* and the *mediatio,* or mediant (semicadence in the middle of the verse). The second half of the verse usually begins on the tenor, which is maintained until the *terminatio,* or final cadence. When the first half of the verse is lengthy, as in verse 4 of this psalm, a *flex* (inflection) serves as a resting point. The mediant and termination are adjusted according to the number of accents of the text, as here in the first verse's mediant of two accents, *cór-de méo,* and the same verse's termination of two accents, *-gá-ti-ó-ne.* The Lesser Doxology usually follows the last verse of the psalm, after which the antiphon is repeated. Originally two choirs alternated in singing the verses of a psalm, a procedure called antiphonal psalmody. Later a soloist chanted the first half of a verse and the choir entered at the asterisk.

f) Antiphon: *Exortum est in tenebris*

EX-ór- tum est * in té-ne- bris   lumen re- ctis corde :

mi-sé-ri-cors et mi-se-rá-tor, et justus Dómi-nus.

Exortum est in tenebris lumen rectis:
   misericors, et miserator, et iustus Dominus.

To the true of heart a light is risen in darkness:
   the Lord is merciful, and compassionate and just.

g) Psalm 111: *Beatus vir qui timet Dominum*

1 Beátus vir qui **tí**met **Dó**minum: *
  in mandátis éjus **vó**let **ní**mis.
2 Pótens in térra érit **sé**men éjus: *
  generátio rectórum be**ne**di**cé**tur.

Blessed is the man that feareth the Lord,
  that delighteth greatly in His commandments.
His seed shall be mighty upon earth;
  the generation of the upright shall be blessed.

3 Glória et divítiae in **dó**mo éjus; ★
   et justítia éjus mánet in sa**é**culum sa**é**culi.

4 Exórtum est in ténebris **lú**men **ré**ctis: ★
   miséricors, et miserátor,
   et **jú**stus.

5 Jucúndus hómo qui miserétur et **cóm**modat,
   † dispónet sermónes súos **in** judício: ★
   quia in aetérnum non **com**movébitur.

6 In memória aetérna **é**rit **jú**stus: ★
   ab auditióne mála **non** timébit.

7 Parátum cor éjus speráre in Dómino,
   † confirmátum**ést** cor éjus: ★
   non commovébitur donec despíciat
   ini**mí**cos **sú**os.

8 Dispérsit, dédit paupéribus:
   † justítia éjus mánet in sa**é**culum saéculi: ★
   córnu éjus exaltábi**tur** in **gló**ria.

9 Peccátor vidébit, et irascétur,
   † déntibus súis frémet **et** ta**bé**scet: ★
   desidérium peccatórum períbit.

10 Glória **Pá**tri, et **Fí**lio, ★
   et Spirítui **Sán**cto.

11 Sicut érat in princípio, et **núnc,**
   et **sém**per, ★ et in saécula saecu**ló**rum. **A**men.

Glory and riches shall be in his house:
   and his righteousness endureth for ever.

Unto the upright there ariseth light in the darkness:
   he is gracious, and full of compassion,
   and righteousness.

Happy is the man that showeth favor and lendeth;
   he will guide his words with discretion:
   surely he shall not be moved for ever.

The righteous shall be in everlasting remembrance.
   He shall not be afraid of evil tidings.

His heart is ready, trusting in the Lord.
   His heart is established,
   he shall not be afraid until he see his desire
   upon his enemies.

He hath dispersed, he hath given to the poor:
   his righteousness endureth for ever:
   his horn shall be exalted with honor.

The wicked shall see it, and be grieved;
   he shall gnash his teeth, and melt away:
   the desire of the wicked shall perish.

Glory be to the Father, and to the Son,
   and to the Holy Ghost.

As it was in the beginning, is now,
   and ever shall be, world without end. Amen.

Return to Antiphon, *Exortum*

h) Antiphon: *Apud Dominum*

A-pud Dóminum * mi-se-ri-córdi-a, et co-pi-ó-sa apud e-um red-émpti-o.

Apud Dominum misericordia, et copiosa apud eum
redemptio.

With the Lord there is mercy, and with Him plentiful
redemption.

i) Psalm 129: *De profundis clamavi ad te*

Mediant of 1 accent
with 2 notes in preparation

De pro-fun-dis cla-ma-vi ad te   Do-mi-ne:

Termination of 1 accent
with 3 preparatory syllables

*Do-mi-ne e-xau-di vo-cem   me-am.

1 De profúndis clamávi *ad te* **Dó**mine: ★
  Dómine exáu*di vócem* **mé**am.

2 Fíant áures túae inten**dén**tes ★
  in vócem depreca*tiónis* **mé**ae.

3 Si iniquitátes observá*veris* **Dó**mine: ★
  Dómine, *quis sustiné*bit?

4 Quia apud te propitiá**tio** est: ★
  et propter légem túam
  sustí*nui te* **Dó**mine.

5 Sustínuit ánima méa in *vérbo* **é**jus: ★
  sperávit ánima *méa in* **Dó**mino.

6 A custódia matutína us*que ad* **nó**ctem, ★
  spéret Is*rael in* **Dó**mino.

7 Quia apud Dóminum mise*ricór*dia: ★
  et copiósa apud *éum red***ém**ptio.

8 Et ípse rédi*met* **Is**rael ★
  ex ómnibus iniqui*tátibus* **é**jus.

9 Glória Pá*tri, et* **Fí**lio, ★
  et Spirí*tui* **Sán**cto.

10 Sicut érat in princípio, *et nunc,*
   et **sém**per, ★ et in saé*cula* sae*culórum.*
   Amen.

Out of the depths I have cried to Thee,
  O Lord! Lord, hear my voice.

Let Thine ears be attentive
  to the voice of my supplication.

If Thou, Lord, shalt observe iniquities,
  Lord, who shall endure it?

For with Thee there is merciful forgiveness,
  and by reason of Thy law
  I have supported Thee, O Lord.

My soul hath relied on His word:
  my soul hath hoped in the Lord.

From the morning watch even until night
  let Israel hope in the Lord.

For with the Lord there is mercy,
  and with Him plentiful redemption.

And He shall redeem Israel,
  from all his iniquities.

Glory be to the Father, and to the Son,
  and to the Holy Ghost.

As it was in the beginning, is now,
  and ever shall be, world without end.
  Amen.

Return to Antiphon, *Apud Dominum*

Psalms 111 and 129 (g, i), each with its antiphon (f, h) and each in a different mode, are sung in the manner just described. After the psalms have been chanted, a biblical passage called the Chapter is read, on this day verses 1–2 of Hebrews 1.

j) Short Responsory: *Verbum caro*

R̷. br.
VI
V Erbum ca- ro factum est, ★ Alle- lú- ia, al- le- lú- ia. Verbum ca- ro factum est, ★ Alle- lú- ia, al-le- lú- ia. ℣. Et ha-bi-tá-vit in no- bis.

* Alle- lú-ia. al- le- lú- ia. ℣. Gló-ri- a Patri, et Fí-li- o, et Spi- rí- tu- i Sancto. Verbum ca- ro factum est, * Alle- lú- ia, al- le- lú- ia.

R. Verbum caro factum est alleluia, alleluia.
V. Et habitavit in nobis. Alleluia, alleluia.
   Gloria Patri, et Filio
   et Spiritui Sancto.

R. The Word was made flesh, alleluia, alleluia.
V. And dwelt among us. Alleluia, alleluia.
   Glory be to the Father, and to the Son,
   and to the Holy Ghost.

The Short Responsory *Verbum caro* is an example of responsorial psalmody, taking the abbreviated form: Respond (choral)—Verse (solo)—Shortened Respond (choral)—Doxology (solo)—Respond (choral). It is called *responsorial* psalmody because a soloist is answered by a choir or congregation.

k) Hymn: *Christe Redemptor omnium*

Christe Red-émptor ómni- um, Ex Patre Patris ú- ni- ce, So-lus ante prin-cí-pi- um Na-tus in-ef-fa- bí- li- ter.

Christe, Redemptor omnium,
Ex Patre, Patris Unice,
Solus ante principium
Natus ineffabiliter

Jesus! Redeemer of the world!
Who, ere the earliest dawn of light,
Was from eternal ages born,
Immense in glory as in might.

Tu lumen, tu splendor Patris,
Tu spes perennis omnium:
Intende, quas fundunt preces.
Tui per orbem famuli.

Memento, salutis Auctor,
Quod nostri quondam corporis,
Ex illibata Virgine
Nascendo, formam sumpseris.

Sic praesens testatur dies,
Currens per anni circulum.
Quod solus a sede Patris
Mundi salus adveneris.

Hunc caelum, terra, hunc mare,
Hunc omne, quod in eis est,
Auctorem adventus tui
Laudans exultat cantico.

Nos quoque, qui sancto tuo,
Redempti sanguine sumus,
Ob diem natalis tui
Hymnum novum concinimus.

Gloria tibi, Domine,
Qui natus es de Virgine,
Cum Patre et Sancto Spiritu
In sempiterna saecula. Amen

Immortal Hope of all mankind
In whom the Father's face we see,
Hear Thou the prayers Thy people pour
This day throughout the world to Thee.

Remember, O Creater Lord!
That in the Virgin's sacred womb
Thou was conceiv'd and of her flesh
Didst our mortality assume.

This ever-blest recurring day
Its witness bears, that all alone,
From Thy own Father's bosom forth,
To save the world Thou camest down.

O Day! to which the seas and sky,
And earth, and heav'n, glad welcome sing;
O Day! which heal'd our misery,
And brought on earth salvation's King.

We, too, O Lord, who have been cleans'd
In Thy own fount of Blood divine,
Offer the tribute of sweet song
On this blest natal day of Thine.

O Jesu! born of Virgin bright,
Immortal glory be to Thee;
Praise to the Father infinite
And Holy Ghost eternally. Amen.

This hymn hails the arrival of the Savior on this day of his birth. Hymns as a genre are strophic—that is, the number of lines, the syllable count, and the meter of all the stanzas are the same. This hymn has seven stanzas of four lines each, each line containing eight syllables and four iambic feet; there is only occasional rhyme. The poetry imitates that of some hymns ascribed to St. Ambrose (d. 397), who was said to have introduced hymns to the Mass, though recent scholarship is inclined to credit this innovation to Hilary, bishop of Poitiers (ca. 315–366). The singing of "hymns, psalms, and spiritual songs" is mentioned by St. Paul (Col. 3:16; Eph. 5:18–20) and other writers of the first three centuries. The setting of this hymn is simple, with no more than two notes per syllable, and it may have been performed rhythmically rather than with the free durations of prose texts and psalms.

l) Verse: *Notum fecit*

℣. No-tum fe-cit Dómi-nus,   alle- lú-ia.

℟. Sa-lu-tá-re su- um, alle- lú- ia.

V. Notum fecit Dominus, alleluia.

R. Salutare suum, alleluia.

V. The Lord hath made known, alleluia.

R. His salvation, alleluia.

Notum fecit is a responsorial recitation of verse fragments from the Gradual for the Mass of Christmas Day, *Viderunt omnes,* with a florid Alleluia refrain.

m) Antiphon: *Hodie Christus natus est* — magnificat

Odi- e * Chri- stus na-tus est : hó-di- e Salvá-tor

appá-ru- it : hó-di- e in terra canunt Ange-li, lætán- tur Ar-

chánge- li : hó-di- e exsúl- tant justi, di-céntes : Gló-ri- a

in excélsis De- o, alle- lú- ia.

Hodie Christus natus est: hodie Salvator paruit: hodie in terra canunt Angeli, laetantur Archangeli: hodie exsultant iusti, dicentes: Gloria in excelsis Deo, alleluia.

This day Christ was born: this day the Savior appeared: this day the Angels sing on earth, and the Archangels rejoice: this day the just exult, saying: Glory to God in the highest, alleluia.

n) Canticle: *Magnificat*

Mediant of 1 accent with 3 preparatory syllables (and an extra note in anticipation of the accent in dactylic cadences).

Endings of 1 accent with 2 preparatory syllables.

Tone 1.   g²

1. Magní- fi-cat *   ánima *mé- a* **Dóminum.**
2. Et exsultávit *spí- ri-tus* mé- us * in Dé- o sa-lu- *tá-ri* mé-   o.

1 Magníficat * ánima *méa* **Dó**minum.	My soul doth magnify the Lord.
2 Et exsultávit *spíritus* **mé**us * in Déo salu*tári* **mé**o.	And my spirit hath rejoiced in God my Savior.
3 Quia respéxit humilitátem *ancíllae* **sú**ae: * ecce enim ex hoc beátam me dícent ómnes gene*rati*ónes.	For he hath regarded the lowliness of His handmaid: for behold from henceforth all generations shall call me blessed.
4 Quia fécit míhi *mágna qui* **pótens** est: * et sánctum *nómen* **é**jus.	For He that is mighty hath done great things to me: and holy is His name.
5 Et misericórdia éjus a progénie *in pro***géni**es * timén*tibus* **é**um.	And His mercy is from generation unto generations, unto them that fear Him.
6 Fécit poténtiam in *bráchio* **sú**o: * dispérsit supérbos ménte *córdis* **sú**i.	He hath showed strength with His arm: He hath scattered the proud in the imagination of their heart.
7 Depósuit po*téntes de* **sé**de, * et exal*távit* **hú**miles.	He hath put down the mighty from their seat, and hath exalted the humble.
8 Esuriéntes *implévit* **bó**nis: * et dívites dim*ísit in***á**nes.	He hath filled the hungry with good things: and the rich He hath sent empty away.
9 Suscépit Israel *púerum* **sú**um, * recordátus misericór*diae* **sú**ae.	He hath received Israel His servant, being mindful of His mercy.
10 Sicut locútus est *ad pátres* **nó**stros, * Abraham et sémini *éjus in* s**aé**cula.	As he spoke to our forefathers, Abraham and to his seed for ever.
11 Glória *Pátri, et* **Fi**lio, * et Spiri*tui* **Sán**cto.	Glory be to the Father, and to the Son, and to the Holy Ghost.
12 Sicut érat in princípio, *et núnc,* et **sém**per, * et in saécula saecu*lórum.* **A**men.	As it was in the beginning, is now, and ever shall be, world without end. Amen.

The Magnificat is the final chant of the Vespers service. Preceded and followed by a timely antiphon, on this occasion *Hodie Christus natus est* (Today Christ is born), it is chanted to a formula very similar to that of the psalms, except that the intonation is sung not only at the outset but at the start of each of the other verses.

GREGORIAN CHANT

Sequence for the Solemn Mass of Easter Day:

Victimae paschali laudes

Seq. 1. Vic - ti - mae pa - scha - li lau - des *im - mo - lent Chri - sti - a - ni.

2. A - gnus red - e - mit o - ves: Chri - stus in - no - cens Pa - tri re - con - ci - li - a - vit pec - ca - to - res.
3. Mors et vi - ta du - el - o con - fli - xe - re mi - ran - do: dux vi - tae mor - tu - us, re - gnat vi - vus.

4. Dic no - bis Ma - ri - a, quid vi - di - sti in vi - a?
5. An - ge - li - cos te - stes, su - da - ri - um, et ve - stes.

Se - pul - crum Chri - sti vi - ven - tis, et glo - ri - am vi - di re - sur - gen - tis:
Sur - re - xit Chri - stus spes me - a: prae - ce - det su - os in Ga - li - lae - am.

[6. Cre - den - dum est ma - gis so - li Ma - ri - ae ve - ra - ci
7. Sci - mus Chri - stum sur - re - xis - se a mor - tu - is ve - re:

quam Ju - dae - o - rum tur - bae fal - la - ci.]
tu no - bis, vi - ctor Rex, mi - se - re - re. A - men. Al - le - lu - ia.

1 Victimae paschali laudes immolent Christiani.

To the Paschal Victim let Christians offer songs of praise.

2 Agnus redemit oves: Christus innocens Patri reconciliavit peccatores.

The Lamb has redeemed the sheep. Sinless Christ has reconciled sinners to the Father.

3 Mors et vita duelo conflixere mirando: dux vitae mortuus, regnat vivus.

Death and life have engaged in miraculous combat. The leader of life is slain, (yet) living he reigns.

4 Dic nobis Maria, quid vidisti in via? Sepulcrum Christi viventis, et gloriam vidi resurgentis:

Tell us, Mary, what you saw on the way? I saw the sepulchre of the living Christ and the glory of His rising;

5 Angleicos testes, sudarium, et vestes. Surexit Christus spes mea: praecedet suos in Galilaeam.

The angelic witnesses, the shroud and vesture. Christ my hope is risen. He will go before his own into Galilee.

Liber usualis, p. 780. Reprinted from Richard Hoppin, *Anthology of Medieval Music* (New York: Norton, 1978), No. 12, p. 15.

6   Credendum est magis soli Mariae veraci
    quam Judaeorum turbae fallaci.

The truthful Mary alone is more to be believed than
    the deceitful crowd of Jews.

7   Scimus Christum surrexisse a mortuis vere:
    tu nobis, victor Rex, miserere

We know that Christ has truly risen from the dead.
    Thou conqueror and king, have mercy on us.

                  —WIPO OF BURGUNDY

                  —Richard Hoppin

Among the many sequences once sung, the celebrated *Victimae paschali laudes* (Praises to the Paschal Victim), is one of only five that are retained in the liturgy and standard modern chant books. It is ascribed to Wipo, chaplain to the Emperor Henry III in the first half of the eleventh century. The classical sequence form of paired strophes is plainly evident, as is the common device of unifying the different melodic segments by similar cadential phrases. Following normal eleventh-century practice, this sequence has an unpaired text at the beginning, but, contrary to the rule, lacks one at the end. Strophe 6, marked by brackets, is omitted in modern chant books, making this sequence conform to the regular pattern.

HILDEGARD OF BINGEN (1098–1179)

Sacred Music Drama: *Ordo virtutum*

In principio omnes

In prin-ci-pi-o om-nes cre-a-tu-ræ

vi-ru-e-runt, in me-di-o flo-res flo-ru-e-runt;

po-ste-a vi-ri-di-tas de-scen-dit. Et is-tud

vir proe-li-a-tor vi-dit et di-xit: Hoc

sci-o, sed au-re-us nu-me-rus non-dum est

ple-nus. Tu er-go, pa-ter-num

spe-cu-lum a-spi-ce: in cor-po-re

me-o fa-ti-ga-ti-o-nem sus-ti-ne-o,

par-vu-li et-i-am me i de-fi-ci-unt.

Nunc me-mor e-sto, quod ple-ni-tu-do quae

in pri-mo fac-ta est a-re-sce-re

non de-bu-it, et tunc in te ha-bu-

VIRTUES

In principio omnes creature viruerunt,
in medio flores floruerunt;
postea viriditas descendit.
Et istud vir proeliator vidit et dixit:
Hoc scio, sed aureus numerus nondum
est plenus. Tu ergo, paternum speculum
aspice: in corpore meo fatigationem
sustineo, parvuli etiam mei deficiunt.
Nunc memor esto, quod plenitudo quae in
primo facta est arescere non debuit, et
tunc in te habuisti quod oculus tuus
numquam cederet usque dum corpus meum
videres plenum gemmarum. Nam me fatigat
quod omnia membra mea in irrisionem
vadunt. Pater, vide, vulnera mea tibi
ostendo.

In the beginning all of creation was
green. In a middle stage the flowers
bloomed. Then greenness declined.
The Fighter [Christ] saw this and said:
"I know this, but the golden number is not
yet attained. You, then, look into the
fatherly mirror. In my body I feel
fatigue, even my little ones weaken.
Be mindful that the fullness that was
first made must not wither, and
make sure that you not turn away your gaze
until you see my body
covered with gems. It wearies me
that all my followers fall into mockery.
Father, behold, I show you my
wounds."

Ergo nunc, omnes homines, genua vestra ad Patrem vestrum flectite, ut vobis manum suam porrigat.	Now, therefore, all humankind, bend your knees before your Father, as he extends his hand to you.

Hildegard, founder and abbess of the convent in Rupertsberg in Germany, was famous for her prophetic powers and revelations. Her most remarkable work, *Scivias* (Know the Ways), is an account of twenty-six visions. Besides writings on natural science and medicine, she left a great quantity of poetry and music.

Her morality play with music, *Ordo virtutum* (The Virtues, ca. 1151), is unusual for its time, because unlike the liturgical dramas such as *Quem quaeritis in praesepe* (NAWM 7), it is not a supplement to the Mass of a certain feast but an independent Latin play, an edifying entertainment for Hildegard's select community of noblewomen. All parts except the Devil are sung in plainchant. The singers represent the Patriarchs and Prophets, sixteen female Virtues (Humility, Love, Obedience, Faith, Hope, Chastity, Innocence, Mercy, etc.), a Happy Soul, an Unhappy Soul, and a Penitent Soul. The Devil, bereft of divine harmony, can only shout and bellow.

The play begins with a chorus of Patriarchs and Prophets who express their wonder at the sight of the richly robed Virtues. Souls in a procession beg the Virtues for divine insight, alternating solos with choral responses. But the Devil tempts the Souls, and one Unhappy Soul succumbs and follows him, only to return later, bedraggled, hurt, and repentant. The Devil tries to reclaim her, but the Virtues, led by Humility, protect her and capture and bind the Devil. Though Victorious, the Virtues lament the spoiling of the green, blossoming paradise and invoke the militant Christ, who urges them to aspire to the goodly fullness of the time of creation.

The final chorus, which serves as an epilogue, consists of four rhymed lines, followed by a prose quotation, and ends with a short prayer. The melody is entirely in Mode 3, keeping mostly to the ambitus of that mode, d′ to e″. It oversteps its upper boundary at "oculus tuus" (your gaze) and "ad Patrem" (to the Father), and its lower boundary at "parvuli" (little ones) and "debuit" (wither), perhaps to emphasize those words. Periods and other strong endings in the text are marked by cadences on the final *E*. The reciting tone of this mode, *C,* plays no part in the structure. Rather the fifth degree, *B,* is the most frequent resting point.

The rhyme of the opening two lines is paralleled by an identical cadence formula in the music, but the next two rhymed lines do not use the same closing pattern, because the second must open the way to Christ's speech. A typical intonation is the rising fifth e′–b′, which occurs at the beginning, at "sed aureus," "non debuit," "Nam me fatigat," "Pater, vide," "Ergo nunc," and "ut vobis." Hildegard, who was sometimes effusive in her melismas, was here restrained, reserving the longer melismas for particular ideas—for example, "debuit" (wither), "gemmarum" (gems), "flectite" (bend), and the longest, a final flourish, for "porrigat" (extend).

7 GREGORIAN CHANT

Trope: *Quem quaeritis in praesepe* (10th century)

In die natale Domini stacio ad Sanctum Petrum

| 19 |

Quem quae - ri - tis in prae - se - pe, pas - to - res, di - ci - te?

3 Respondent

Sal - va - to - rem, Chri - stum Do - mi - num, in - fan - tem pan - nis in - vo - lu - tum,

se - cun - dum ser - mo - nem an - ge - li - cum.

Ad - est hic par - vu - lus cum Ma - ri - a, ma - tre su - a, de qua du - dum

va - ti - ci - nan - do I - sa - i - as di - xe - rat pro - phe - ta: Ec - ce vir - go con - ci - pi - et

et pa - ri - et fi - li - um; et nunc e - un - tes di - ci - te qui - a na - tus est.

Respondent

Al - le - lu - ia, al - le - lu - ia! Iam ve - re sci - mus Chri - stus na - - tum in ter - ris, de quo

ca - ni - te o - mnes cum pro - phe - ta di - cen - tes, PU - ER NA - TUS EST NO - BIS.

In die natale Domini stacio ad Sanctum Petrum	On the day of the nativity of the Lord, at the station of St. Peter
Incipiunt tropus [i.e. tropum] antequam dicatur officium	They begin the trope before the office [i.e. Introit] is said

Transcribed from Paris, Bibliothèque nationale, MS lat. 1118, fols. 8v–9r (MS datable 988–96), by William L. Smoldon in *The Music of the Medieval Church Dramas.* © The estate of the late W. L. Smoldon, 1980.

Quem quaeritis in praesepe,
pastores, dicite?

Respondent
Salvatorem, Christum Dominum,
infantem pannis involutum,
secundum sermonem angelicum.

Adest hic parvulus cum Maria,
matre sua, de qua dudum
vaticinando Isaias dixerat propheta:
Ecce virgo concipiet et
pariet filium; et nun euntes
dicite quia natus est.

Respondent
Alleluia, alleluia!
Iam vere scimus Christu natum
in terris, de quo canite omnes
cum propheta dicentes,
PUER NATUS EST NOBIS.

Whom do you seek in the manger,
shepherds, please say?

Our savior, Christ the Lord,
an infant wrapped in cloths,
according to the angelic report.

The infant is attended here by Mary,
his mother, about whom a little while
ago the prophet Isaiah foretold:
behold a virgin will conceive and
give birth to a son; and now as you go
tell that he is born.

Alleluia, alleluia!
Now truly we know that Christ was born
on earth, concerning which sing always
with the prophet, saying:
A SON IS BORN UNTO US.

The rubrics indicate that this dramatic dialogue was performed before the singing of the Introit at the Third Mass of Christmas Day at the altar which symbolized the Church of Saint Peter.

Certain chants, usually Introits, were extended by a verbal and melodic trope that turned them into little dramatic scenes. Best known is the Easter trope, *Quem quaeritis in sepulcro?*, in which the angels guarding Jesus' tomb ask the two Marys, "Whom do you seek in the sepulchre?" They answer, "Jesus of Nazareth, who was crucified." The angels tell them that he is not there, for he has risen. This genre is sometimes called a liturgical drama.

Quem quaeritis in praesepe is the Christmas version of the dramatic Easter trope. The midwives caring for the Christ child ask the shepherds to tell them whom they seek in the manger. The shepherds answer that they are looking for an infant in swaddling clothes, Christ the Savior, as the angels foretold. The angels explain that the child was born to Mary, a virgin. The shepherds rejoice in the knowledge that they have confirmed the birth of Christ. The Introit, *Puer natus est* (NAWM 3a), is then sung.

There are a number of notable melodic recurrences in this dialogue. The music of the first response (marked "Respondent") parallels that of the midwives, except that its phrase ends a fifth above, because the speech continues. The previous phrases all ended with the same cadence, G–A–G–F–G. But the first shepherd's last words, "sermonem angelicum," introduce a new ending formula that will be repeated at "Isaias dixerat propheta" of the second response and "propheta dicentes" of the third. The last four notes of this formula are heard again at the end of the second response at "natus est." Although different characters are singing, the melodic recurrences bestow melodic continuity and unity on the entire composition.

8 ADAM DE LA HALLE (CA. 1237–CA. 1287)

Jeu de Robin et de Marion

Rondeau: *Robins m'aime*

Robins m'aime,	Robin loves me,
Robins m'a,	Robin has me,
Robins m'a demandée	Robin asked me
Si m'ara.	if he can have me.
Robins m'acata cotele	Robin bought me a skirt
D'escarlate bonne et belle	of scarlet, good and pretty,
Souskanie et chainturele.	a bodice and belt.
Aleuriva!	Hurray!

The most famous of the secular musical plays was *Jeu de Robin et de Marion* by Adam de la Halle, the last and greatest of the trouvères. It is uncertain whether all the songs in this work, dating from about 1284, were written by Adam himself or whether they were popular chansons incorporated into the play. A few of them have polyphonic settings.

Typical of the tuneful songs is *Robins m'aime,* sung by Marion with choral refrains at the opening of the *Jeu.* It is a monophonic rondeau in the form ABaabAB (using separate letters for each musical phrase, capitals for choral, lower case for solo performance).

Friedrich Gennrich, *Troubadours, Trouvères, Minne- und Meistergesang* (Cologne, 1951) p. 38.

BERNART DE VENTADORN (CA. 1150– CA. 1180)

9

Can vei la lauzeta mover

Can vei la lauzeta mover
de joi sas alsas contral rai,
que s'oblid' e·s laissa chazer
per la doussor c'al cor li vai,
ai! tan grans enveya m'en ve
de cui qu'eu veya jauzion,
meravilhas ai, car desse
lo cor de dezirer no·m fon.

Ai, las! tan cuidava saber
d'amor, e tan petit en sai,
car eu d'amar no·m posc tener
celeis don ja pro non aurai.
Tout m'a mo cor, e tout m'a me,
e se mezeis e tot lo mon;
e can se·m tolc, no·m laisset re
mas dezirer e cor volon.

Anc non agui de me poder
ni no fui meus de l'or' en sai
que·m laisset en sos olhs vezer

en un miralh que mout me plai.
Mirahls, pus me mirei en te,
m'an mort li sospir depreon,
c'aissi·m perdei com perdet se
lo bels Narcisus en la fon.

When I see the lark beating
its wings joyfully against the sun's rays,
which then swoons and swoops down
because of the joy in its heart,
oh! I feel such jealousy
for all those who have the joy of love,
that I am astonished
that my heart does not immediately melt with desire!

Alas! I thought I knew so much
of love, and I know so little;
for I cannot help loving a lady
from whom I shall never obtain any favor.
She has taken away my heart and myself,
and herself and the whole world;
and when she left me, I had nothing left
but desire and a yearning heart.

I have no power over myself,
and have not had possession of myself
since the time when she allowed me to look into
    her eyes,
in a mirror which I like very much.
Mirror, since I was reflected in you,
deep sighs have killed me,
for I caused my own ruin, just as
fair Narcissus caused his by looking in the fountain.

Text and translation are from Hendrik van der Werf, *The Chansons of the Troubadours and Trouvères* (Utrecht, 1972), pp. 91–95, where versions of the melody appearing in five different sources are given, showing surprising consistency among readings. The dot splitting two letters of a word, as in e·s, indicates a contraction.

39

De las domnas me dezesper;
ja mais en lor no·m fiarai;
c'aissi com las solh chaptener,
enaissi las deschaptenrai.
Pois vei c'una pro no m'en te
vas leis que·m destrui e·m confon,
totas las dopt' e las mescre,
car be sai c'atretals se son.

D'aisso's fa be femna parer
ma domna, par qu'e·lh o retrai,
car no vol so c'om deu voler,
e so c'om li devada, fai.
Chazutz sui en mala merce,
et ai be faih co·l fols en pon;
e no sai per que m'esdeve,
mas car trop puyei contra mon.

Merces es perduda, per ver,
et eu non o saubi anc mai,
car cilh qui plus en degr'aver
no·n a ges, et on la querrai?
A! can mal sembla, qui la ve,
qued aquest chaitiu deziron

que ja ses leis non aura be,
laisse morir, que no l'aon!

Pus ab midons no·m pot valer
precs ni merces ni·l dreihz qu'eu ai,
ni a leis no ven a plazer
qu'eu l'am, ja mais no·lh o dirai.
Aissi·m part de leis e·m recre;
mort m'a, e per mort h respon,
e van m'en, pus ilh no·m rete,
chaitius, en issilh, no sai on.

Tristans, ges no·m auretz de me,
qu'eu m'en vau, chaitius, no sai on.
De chantar me gic e·m recre,
e de joi d'amor m'escon.

I despair of ladies;
I shall not trust them ever again;
just as I used to defend them,
now I shall condemn them.
Since I see that *one* of them does not help me
against her who is ruining and destroying me
I fear them all and have no faith in them,
for I know they are all the same.

My lady shows herself to be [merely] a woman
(and that is why I reproach her)
in that she does not want what one should want,
and she does what is forbidden her.
I have fallen out of favor,
and have acted like the fool on the bridge;
and I do not know why this has happened to me,
unless it was because I tried to climb too high.

Mercy is gone, that is sure,
and I never received any of it,
for she who should have the most mercy
has none, and where else should I seek it?
Oh! how difficult it is for a person who sees her
to imagine that she would allow to die this poor
        yearning wretch,
and would not help the man
who can have no help but her!

Since pleas and mercy and my rights
cannot help me to win my lady,
and since it does not please her
that I love her, I shall speak to her about it no more.
So I am leaving her and her service;
she has killed me, and I reply with death,
and I am going sadly away, since she will not accept
my service, into exile, I do not know where.

Tristan, you will hear no more of me,
for I am going sadly away, I do not know where,
I am going to stop singing,
and I flee from love and joy.

One of the best-preserved songs by the troubadour Bernart de Ventadorn is a lover's complaint, the main subject of the entire repertory. The song is strophic, each stanza but the last having eight lines rhymed a b a b c d c d, and each line has eight syllables. The music to which all the stanzas are sung is through-composed, though the seventh line partly repeats the fourth. The melody is clearly in first mode, rising from *d* to *a* in the first phrase and from *a* to *d'* in the second and third.

BEATRIZ DE DIA (D. CA. 1212)

Canso: *A chantar*

1. A chan-tar m'es al cor que non deu-ri - e
2. tant mi ran-cun cele a qui sui a - migs,
3. et si l'am mais que nu - le ren qui si - e;
4. non mi val ren bel - tat ni cur - te-si - e
5. ne ma bon-taz ne mon pres ne mon sen;
6. al - tre - si sui en - ga - nade et tra - gi - de
7. qu'e - u - sse fait vers lui de - sa - vi - nen - ce.

A chantar m'es al cor que non deurie
tant mi rancun cele a qui sui amigs,
et si l'am mais que nule ren qui sie;
non mi val ren beltat ni curtesie
ne ma bontaz ne mon pres ne mon sen;
altresi sui enganade et tragide
qu'eusse fait vers lui desavinence.

To sing I must of what I'd rather not,
so much does he of whom I am the lover embitter me;
yet I love him more than anything in the world.
To no avail are my beauty or politeness,
my goodness, or my virtue and good sense.
For I have been cheated and betrayed,
as if I had been disagreeable to him.

In this strophic song, or *canso,* from the second half of the twelfth century, four distinct melodic components are arranged in the form ABABCDB. All lines but one end on an unaccented syllable, a circumstance emphasized

Transcribed by Hendrik van der Werf in *The Extant Troubadour Melodies* (Rochester: Author, 1984), p. 13. Gerald A. Bond, text editor. Used by permission.

by the triple notes of the penultimate syllable. The melody is clearly in the first mode, with the characteristic fifth, $d'-a'$, and final, d', of this mode displayed in the A and B phrases. As in first-mode plainchant melodies, it descends one note below the final to c'. The singer was presumed to vary the melody for each new stanza, holding to the outline of the tune.

A *vida,* or biographical tale, of about a century later tells that "Beatrix, comtessa de Dia, was a beautiful and good woman, the wife of Guillaume de Poitiers. And she was in love with Rambaud d'Orange and made about him many good and beautiful songs." It is not known which parts of this account are legendary and which are true.

WIZLAU VON RÜGEN (CA. 1268–1325)

We ich han gedacht

We ich han gedacht
Al disen nacht
An mine grozen swere.
De eyn wip beghat,
Unde mich nicht lat
Komen tzü eyner were,
Daz se mir wolde nahen:
Eyn cusselin
Uz ir munt ist phin,
Den wolde ich wol untphahen.

Vil süze vrucht,
Wer daz din tzucht,
Daz du mich wult vürterben?
Wer gnade socht,
Unn der an dir rocht,
Dem solt du selde erben.
Daz were an mime rate,
Daz du minnen phant
In sine hant
Ghebest uz dines hertzen grate.

Waz ich ye ghesanc,
Nie mir ghelanc
An diner hohen minne;
Des lide ich not.
Eyn irren tot,
Den ich davon ghewinne.

Alas, I have been thinking
this whole night
of my great burdens,
which a woman begot
and which do not allow me
to feel at all secure
that she might want to approach me:
a little kiss
from her mouth is a lovely thing,
which I would gladly accept.

Such a sweet creature,
with all your fine breeding:
yet you want to destroy me?
On him who seeks affection
and hopes for it from you
you ought to bestow happiness.
This would be my advice:
that you give love's pledge
in his hand
from your heart's midst.

Whatever I sang,
I never rose
to your noble love:
therefore I suffer distress,
a stray death,
which I thereby achieve.

Transcribed from the neumatic notation in Gregor Holz, Franz Saran, and Eduard Bernoulli, *Die Jenaer Liederhandschrift* (Leipzig, 1901), I, 130.

Imer wil ich dich bitten:
Mir hilft keyn rat,
Also mir nu stat
In minem hertzen mitten.

Always will I come begging to you.
No advice will help me,
as I now feel
in my heart's midst.

In this song by Prince Wizlau von Rügen, the *Weise,* or melodic pattern, for singing the ten-line stanzas has a musical form that is even more repetitive than the rhyme scheme:

Rhyme   a a b/ c c b/ d e e d
Melody   A A B/ A A B/ C A A B

HANS SACHS (1494–1576)

12

Nachdem David war redlich und aufrichtig

24

Nachdem David war redlich und aufrichtig,
In allen sachen treu als golde,
Do wart jm Saul gar neidig;
Rett mit all seinen knechten in gedulde.
Sprach:"er würgt David heimlich, gar fürsichtig."
Doch war Jonathan David holde;
Dem wars von herzen leide,
Das jhn Saul wollte töten ohn alle schulde.

David Er das ansaget,
Sprach:"mein Vater radschlaget,
Wie Er dich heimlich thu ermören.

Since David was honest and candid,
in all things true as gold,
so Saul was very jealous of him.
He dealt with all his vassals with patience.
Said he:"He struggled with David secretly, cautiously.
Yet Jonathan was kind to David;
it was painful to his heart
that Saul wanted to kill him [David] without
　　any blame.
Thus he spoke to David:
saying, "My father turned a somersault,
when he secretly [planned] to murder you;

Adapted from diplomatic copy in G. Münzer, *Das Singebuch des Adam Puschman* (Leipzig, 1906),
p. 80. Notation in whole and half notes, some with dots, is in the original manuscript in Wrocław,
Municipal Library. Half notes are meant to go much faster than whole notes. Dotted half notes are
somewhat prolonged. Puschamn labels this *Weise,* or melodic formula, "Klingender Ton" (chiming or
ringing mode).

Darumb auff morgen,
So bleib verborgen,
Versteck dich auf dem felde."
So wiel ich reden von dem handel wichtig,
Was ich vom Vater den wertt hören,
Ich dir treu vermelde,
Ob bey ihm sey feintschaft oder hulde.

therefore in the morning
remain concealed,
hide yourself in the field."
As much as I tell of the affair is important;
what I, concerning the father's honor, heard,
I truthfully impart,
whether there was hostility in him or kindness.

Hans Sachs, a shoemaker by trade, is the most celebrated of the Meistersinger, partly because Wagner made him a leading character in *Die Meistersinger von Nürnberg*. Of the many fine examples of Sachs's art that survive, one of the most beautiful is this commentary on the strife between David and Saul (1 Samuel 17ff.). It is in a form common in the Minnelied that was taken over by the Meistersinger, called in German *Bar* form. The same melodic period, A, is set to a stanza's first two units of text (called *Stollen*), and a different and usually longer melodic period, B (called *Abgesang*), is set to the remainder of the stanza, resulting in the pattern A A B. This form was also the basis of the Provençal *canzo*; like the canzo, the Bar form sometimes involves a repeat of all or part of the Stollen phrase toward the end of the Abgesang. This is the case in *Nachdem David*, where the entire melody of the Stollen is reiterated at the end of the Abgesang.

Istampita Palamento

13

Jen ten Bokum, *De Dansen* (Utrecht, 1976), pp. 49–50. Facsimile in Gilbert Reaney, ed., *The Manuscript London, British Museum, Additional 29987* (American Institute of Musicology, 1965), fols. 60r–61v.

The *istampita* (French: *estampie*; Provençal: *estampida*) was a textless composition perhaps intended for dancing. Its form, which resembles that of the sequence, consists of sections immediately repeated (double versicles), often with open and closed endings.

This istampita has five *partes*. The *prima pars* shows the form more clearly than the rest of the piece. The same music is heard twice, the first time with an open (*aperto*) ending, the second time with a closed (*chiuso*) ending. The second and third partes use the same two endings and, in addition, borrow the sixteen previous measures from the first pars. The fourth and fifth partes share the same music except for the first eight measures and, of course, the open and closed endings. Some of the later partes borrow material from earlier partes. These borrowings, indicated in the manuscripts and most editions by *signa congruentiae*, have been written out in this transcription to make it easier to follow the recorded performance.

(In two short segments the players in the recording improvise rather than read from the written score: Quarta pars, measures 34–37; Quinta pars, measures 45–52.)

14 Organum: *Alleluia Justus ut palma*

Alleluia Justus ut palma florebit,
et sicut cedrus multiplicabitur.

Alleluia. The righteous shall flourish
like a palm tree and shall multiply like a cedar.

This organum serves as an example in *Ad organum faciendum*, a treatise on how to make organum preserved in a manuscript from around 1100 at the Ambrosian Library in Milan (MS M.17 sup.). An organal voice is set mostly note-against-note above the plainchant Alleluia (but occasionally crossing below). The text of the verse is *Justus ut palma*. The example exhibits both contrary and parallel motion from one interval to the next. There is contrary motion from octaves or unisons to fourths or fifths, particularly at the beginning of a phrase. Within a phrase fourths or fifths or mixtures of these may move in parallel. Particularly at the end of a phrase, a fourth or fifth proceeds to a unison or octave. The composer also discovered that moving from a sixth to an octave or from a third to a unison was an effective cadential device.

Milan, Biblioteca Ambrosiana, MS M. 17 sup., ed. Hans Heinrich Eggebrecht and Frieder Zaminer, *Ad organum faciendum, Lehrschriften der Mehrstimmigkeit in nachguidonischer Zeit* (Mainz, 1970), p. 53.

MAGISTER ALBERTUS OF PARIS (?)

Benedicamus Domino Trope: *Congaudeant catholici*

Con-gau-de — ant ca-tho-li — ci, le-ten-tur ci — ves ce-li — ci

di — e i — — — —

— — — sta.

De-o di-ca-mus gra — ti — a

(The spelling of the Latin text has been standardized.)

Congaudeant catholici,	Let us all rejoice together,
Laetentur cives caelici	let the heavenly hosts be glad
Die ista.	on this day.
Clerus pulchris carminibus	Let the clergy attend to pretty poems
Studeat atque cantibus	and songs
Die ista.	on this day.
Haec est dies laudabilis	This is a praiseworthy day,
Divina luce nobilis	noble in the divine light
Die ista.	on this day.
Vincens Herodis gladium,	Winning the sword of Herod,
Accepit vitae bravium	may he have the life of the brave
Die ista.	on this day.
Qua Jacobus palatia	[The day] that Jacob
Ascendit ad caelestia	ascends to the celestial palaces
Die ista.	on this day.

Transcribed from the Codex Calixtinus, fol. 185, at the Cathedral of Santiago de Compostela. For a facsimile of the original manuscript, see HWM, p. 78. For rhythmic interpretations, see Gustave Reese, *Music in the Middle Ages*, p. 268, and Theodore Karp, *The Polyphony of Saint Martial and Santiago de Compostela* (Oxford: Clarendon Press, 1992), 2:206.

Ergo carenti termino Benedicamus Domino die ista.	Therefore without limit let us praise the Lord on this day.
Magno patri familias Solvamus laudis gratias die ista.	To the great head of the family let us give thanks with praise on this day.
Deo dicamus gratia.	Let us say thanks to God.

A repertory of organum found in the Aquitanian region consisted mainly of tropes to the *Benedicamus Domino*, a chant used both in Offices and the Mass. The texts of these tropes are rhymed, metrical, accentual Latin poems. Such a trope, *Congaudeant catholici*, is preserved in a manuscript at the Cathedral of Santiago de Compostela, on the northern coast of Spain, one of the favorite pilgrimage destinations in the Middle Ages. It is attributed in this manuscript to Magister Albertus of Paris, who was cantor at the Cathedral of Notre Dame and active there between about 1146 and 1177. The poem consists of eight rhymed couplets, each line having eight syllables, in a sometimes forced iambic accentual meter. A four-syllable refrain follows each couplet. The musical setting is typical in that the uppermost part often has a burst of melody on the penultimate syllable of a word. These melismas take off from consonances in which the three parts meet. On the other hand, this trope is unusual in that a melismatic organum is superimposed on a two-part note-against-note organum which is, at the refrain "Die ista," itself a melismatic duet.

This trope is believed to be the oldest preserved three-part piece. The notation does not permit a consistent rhythmic interpretation of the uppermost part or a positive lining up of that part with the lower two. The manuscript does not indicate any flats.

Alleluia Pascha nostrum

Gregorian Chant and Early Polyphonic Elaborations

To permit comparison of how plainchant settings were variously embellished in the twelfth and thirteenth centuries, several polyphonic versions of the *Alleluia Pascha nostrum* are given here. They are presented as they could have been performed in the thirteenth century, when more elaborate settings of certain sections replaced simple organum, just as simple organum replaced sections of plainchant. The series of pieces follows, in performance order.

a) Plainchant [not performed separately on the recording]

Gordon A. Anderson, *The Latin Compositions in Fascicules VII and VIII of the Notre Dame Manuscript Wolfenbüttel Helmstedt 1099*, Part II, p. 276. Réproduit avec permission de l'institut de musique medié-vale, Henriville, Ottawa et Binningen.

b) Léonin (fl. 1163–1190), Organum duplum

Florence, Biblioteca Medicea-Laurenziana, MS Pluteus 29.1, fol. 109; the clausulae are from Anderson, II 25–26.

c) Anonymous clausula on *nostrum* (not heard on the recording)

[combined in one score with]

d) Texted motet: *Gaudeat devotio fidelium*

[The texted duplum of the motet, which is based on the duplum of the clausula, is heard over the *nostrum* tenor.]

um. Vi - te pan - dit o - sti - um, Dum mor - tis sup - pli - ci - um, Pi - e to - le -

rat. Mun - di prin - ceps ex - tur - ba - tur, Dum con - si - de - rat,

II

Quod per mor - tem li - be - ra - tur Qui per - i - e - rat, Iu - re su - o sic pri - va - tur,

Dum de - si - derat Il - lum si - bi sub - de - re, qui nil com - mi - se - rat.

d) Gaudeat devotio fidelium;

Verbum patris incarnatur,
Nova proles nobis datur
Et nobis cum conversatur
Salus gentium.
Vite pandit ostium,
Dum mortis supplicium,
Pie tolerat.

Let the devotion of the faithful be raised in
rejoicing;
the word of the father is made flesh,
and a new child is given to us,
and He has bestowed Himself upon us.
The salvation of the people
has opened the gateway of life,
for he in devotion has borne
the punishment of death.

Mundi princeps exturbatur,	Satan was cast down
Dum considerat,	when He stood firm
Quod per morten liberatur	so that through His death
Qui perierat.	he who had perished might be made free;
Iure suo sic privatur,	thus was He stripped of His own devine nature
Dum desiderat	when He chose
Illum sibi subdere, qui nihil commiserat.	to subdue death unto Himself—He who had committed no sin.

[Léonin organum continues]

e) Substitute clausula on *la* of the word *immolatus*

[combined in one score with]

f) Motet: *Ave Maria, Fons letitie,* on the same tenor *la*

[The textless clausula is not heard; the almost identical motet is performed on the recording.]

f) Ave Maria.	Hail Mary,
Fons letitie,	fount of Joy,
Virgo pura, pia,	virgin pure and holy,
Vas munditie,	vessel of chastity,
Te voce varia	may the joyous people
Sonet sobrie	sing Thee in various
Gens leta sobria.	yet restrained voices.
Gaudens varie	Rejoicing for many blessings,
Promat ecclesia	let the Church express
Laudes Marie,	its praise for Mary;
Vox ecclesie.	and let the voice of the Church
Sonet in maria.	resound in the sea.
Hec solvit scrinia	She has fulfilled the prophecies
Ysaie,	of Isaiah,
Reserans ostia	unlocking the once-closed
Clausa patrie,	gates of heaven,
Via dans eximia	granting access by a wonderful way
Regem glorie,	to the King of Glory,
Qui sola gratia,	who by grace alone,
Plenus gratie,	and full of grace,
Factus est hostia,	was made sacrifice,
Finis hostie.	the end of all sacrifice.

—Adapted from Anderson, II, 52–53

[Léonin organum continues]

g) Motet: *Salve, salus hominum / O radians stella / nostrum*, a double-texted motet on the tenor *nostrum*.

TRIPLUM

g) Salve, salus hominum,   Hail, safety of men,
   Spes misericordie,   hope of pity,
   Spes venie,   hope of pardon,
   Purgatrix criminum,   cleanser of sins,
   Cecis lumen luminum,   light of light to the blind,
   Mater prudentie,   Mother of prudence,
   Signum vie,   sign-post of the way,
   Terminus patrie,   boundary of Heaven,
   Spes venie,   hope of pardon,
   Nectar, flos glorie,   nectar, flower of glory,
   Iustitie   of justice,
   Sol pie,   holy sun,
   Clementie   of tranquillity
   Sobrie   of prudence
   Ros, virgo munditie.   dew, Virgin of cleanliness!
                                              —Adapted from Anderson, II, 324.

DUPLUM

O radians stella pre ceteris,   O shining star, outshining all others,
Summi Dei mater et filia,   Mother and Daughter of the highest God,
Eximia proles degeneris,   peerless offspring of a degenerate race,
Tu generis Mundi letitia,   Thou art the joy of the people of the world.
Tu de via tribulos conteris,   Thou turnest away the perils of the way.
Spes miseris,   O hope of wretched
Hominis   humanity;
Nescia Maria   Mary, not knowing [the touch of man],
De lateris luto nos libera,   free us from the mire surrounding us,
Regenerans genus in posteris regia.   regenerating the human race in thy kingdom for
                                           all ages.

When the Alleluia was performed as plainchant, it was sung by a priest, who was joined at certain points by a unison chorus. The priest began by intoning the word "Alleluia," after which the chorus repeated this initial segment of melody. The chorus then continued until the priest intervened with the Verse, a line from one of the psalms. Toward the end of the Verse, the chorus joined in and completed the Verse. The soloist and chorus then repeated the entire Alleluia.

While Léonin set the solo sections polyphonically, comparison of his setting (16b) with the original chant (16a) makes it evident that he expected the sections normally sung by the chorus to remain simple plainsong. The plan of Léonin's organum may be diagrammed as follows:

Soli	Chorus	Soli
Organum duplum (16b)	Plainchant	Organum duplum (16b cont.)
Alleluia _____	*Alleluia* ____	*Pascha* _____

Soli cont.		
Discant clausula (16c)	Organum duplum (16b cont.)	Substitute clausula (16e)
no-strum (melisma)___	*immo-la-* _____	(melisma) *tus* (melisma) *est* ___

Chorus	Soli		Chorus
Plainchant	Org. dupl. (16b cont.)	Discant (16b cont.)	Plainchant
Christus. ___	*Alle-* _____	*lu-ia.* _____	

The formal and sonorous contrast already present in the responsorial plainchant performance is thus magnified. The different styles of setting build further contrast into the polyphonic sections. The opening intonation "Alleluia" (16b) resembles the older melismatic or florid organum: the plainsong intonation (transposed down a fifth) is stretched out into unmeasured long notes of indefinite duration to form the tenor; against this a solo voice sings textless melismatic phrases, broken at irregular intervals by cadences and rests. The original notation suggests a free, unmeasured rhythm. The fluid melody—non-periodic and loosely segmented—strongly suggests improvisatory practice. Nevertheless, some scholars have applied the patterns of the rhythmic modes to such passages of organum purum, and their transcriptions are seen in many editions and heard on some recordings. The transcription given here assumes unmeasured rhythm for these passages.

After the chorus responds "Alleluia" in unison, the two-voice solo texture resumes with the psalm verse on the word "Pascha." But beginning with the word "nostrum" a quite different style is heard (16c). The tenor now sings in strictly measured rhythm; the upper voice, which moves in faster notes, like-wise assumes the distinctly measured character of discant, the style in which all parts are in measured rhythm. Section 16c constitutes a *clausula*, a closed form in discant style in which a chant melisma is heard twice in the tenor (the two appearances of the tenor are marked by Roman numerals I and II). (See the facsimile in HWM of the page from the Florence manuscript containing this clausula.)

The choice of whether to use organum or discant style was not a matter of caprice. It was based on the general principle that in those portions of the original chant that were syllabic or only slightly florid—where compara-tively few notes were sung to a syllable—the organal style with long sus-tained tones in the tenor was appropriate. In those portions, however, where the original chant was itself highly melismatic, it was necessary for the tenor to move along more quickly, so that the whole piece would not be length-ened unduly. Instead of many notes in the added part to each note in the chant, the discant clausula counterposed two to four notes to each note of a melisma.

In the Florentine source from which 16b, c, and d are taken, this Alleluia has three clausulae: on *nostrum*, as we saw; on *latus* of the word "immolatus"; and on *lu* of the final "Alleluia." Between these clausulae there are contrast-ing sections in organum purum style. After the last discant section, the cho-rus closes the piece with the concluding few phrases of the plainsong Alleluia on which the composition is based.

In both organum purum and discant, the attack of a new tenor note is normally accompanied by a consonance in the other parts, the longer such notes by a perfect consonance. At the close of extended sections, such as at *lu* and *ia* of "Alleluia," at *no* of "nostrum," or at *est*, a second may move to a unison or a seventh to an octave in what resembles a modern appoggiatura. The discant sections are additionally organized through rests, which break up the melodies into easily grasped phrases.

Clausulae such as 16c were sometimes converted into motets by the addition of texts in Latin, French, or both. For example, setting a Latin text, *Gaudeat devotio fidelium*, to the duplum turned the clausula on *nostrum* (16c) into a motet (16d).

Similarly, the clausula on *latus* (16e) became a motet in honor of the Virgin, *Ave Maria, Fons letitie* (16f). The brevity of the clausula's musical phrases in the duplum obliged the poet to invent rhyming endings for every second line.

A clausula on *nostrum* different from 16c is behind the duplum of the motet in 16g. This duplum received the text *O radians stella pre ceteris* to form a two-part motet. At a later stage a third part, or triplum, was added, with the text *Salve salus hominum*, making it a three-part motet. The two poetic texts are unrelated to the Alleluia verse but complement each other in that they are addressed to the Virgin. The texts were set to the music, rather than the other way around, so their line lengths are irregular, and the rhyme scheme is extremely simple, alternating two syllables, "is" and "ia" in the duplum, "um" and "ie" in the triplum. The third rhythmic mode of the triplum matches that of the duplum, but the lengths of the phrases are calculated to avoid simultaneous rests. This motet was also converted to secular uses by having a French text substituted for each of the upper parts, namely *Qui d'amors veut bien* in the triplum and *Qui longuement porroit* in the duplum. As in the Latin motet, the two texts reinforced each other and each used only two different rhyming syllables.

17 PÉROTIN (FL. 1180–CA. 1238)

Organum quadruplum: *Sederunt*

Gradual for St. Stephen's Day

Reprinted from Hoppin, *Anthology of Medieval Music* (New York: Norton, 1978), No. 35, pp. 59–66.
For a facsimile of the original notation of the end of the *Sederunt* section, see HWM, p. 87.

de -

runt.

Chorus

prin - ci - pes,   et ad-ver-sum me   lo - que - ban - tur:

et in - i - qui per-se - cu - ti   sunt me.

Sederunt principes,
et adversum me loquebantur;
et iniqui persecuti sunt me.

The rulers were seated in council,
and they spoke against me;
and my enemies persecuted me.

—Richard Hoppin

This organum is the music for the intonation (the first word) of the Respond of the Gradual for St. Stephen's Day. It is a portion of a very long composition that must have taken about twenty minutes to perform. Since the text did not provide a means of organizing the music, the composer resorted to abstract, purely musical devices. One of these is voice exchange. In measures 13–18 the duplum and triplum exchange two-measure motives, while the quadruplum sounds the same pattern three times, like an ostinato.

The duplum and quadruplum have a similar exchange in measures 24 to 29. Meanwhile there is a more extended line traded between the quadruplum, measures 13–23, and the triplum, measures 24–34. Simultaneously measures 13–23 of the duplum are equivalent to the quadruplum's measures 24–34. In effect, therefore, measures 24–34 sound the same as measures 13–23. The large-scale interchange must have made the music more interesting to the singers, but listeners would simply have heard an eleven-measure section repeated. Shorter voice exchanges occur throughout the "Sederunt" section, and there is also motive repetition within a single voice. Particularly notable are the coupling of phrases that are nearly alike, such as measures 131–134 and 135–138, which exhibit an antecedent-consequent relationship. Johannes de Garlandia, who wrote a treatise on the rhythm of the Notre Dame usage, remarked that complementary phrases of this kind occurred particularly in a style of organum called copula, which he said was intermediate between discant and organum purum. Measures 109–112 and 113–116 are similarly related and, in addition, contain voice exchanges.

Conductus: *Ave virgo virginum*

A - ve vir - go vir - gi - num   Ver - bi car - nis cel - la,

In sa - lu - tem ho - mi - num   Stil - lans lac et mel - la.

Pe - pe - ri - sti do - mi - num,   Mo - y - si fi - cel - la,

O ra - di - o Sol ex - it,   et lu - mi - num,   fon - tem pa - rit stel - la.

Ave virgo virginum
Verbi carnis cella,
In salutem hominum
Stillans lac et mella.
Peperisti dominum,
Moysi ficella,
O radio
Sol exit, et luminum
Fontem parit stella.

Hail, virgin of virgins,
shrine of the word made flesh,
who for man's salvation
drips milk and honey.
You bore the Lord;
you were a rush-basket for Moses;
O, from your rays
the sun goes forth, and the star
brings forth a fountain of light.

Florence, Biblioteca Laurenziana, MS Pluteus 29.1, fol. 240r–240v.

Ave, plena gratia,	Hail, full of grace,
Caput Zabulonis	chief of Zebulun,
Contrivisti spolia	the spoils of robbers
Reparans predonis.	you restore.
Celi rorans pluvia	Like rain, falling from heaven
Vellus Gedeonis,	on the fleece of Gideon,
O filio	with your son
Tu nos reconcilia,	reunite us,
Mater Salomonis.	O mother of Solomon!
Virgo tu mosayce	You, Virgin,
Rubus visionis,	bramble-bush of the Mosaic vision,
De te fluxit sylice	from you flowed the fountain
Fons redemptionis.	through the rock of redemption.
Quos redemit calice	Those Christ has redeemed through the chalice
Christus passionis,	of his passion,
O gaudio	O, may he clothe them with the joy
Induat glorifice	of his glorious
Resurrectionis	resurrection.

Like so much of the Latin poetry of this period, this thirteenth-century conductus is addressed to the Virgin Mary and was probably used in special devotions and processions. Three strophes are served by the same music, and, besides, the first two couplets have identical music in all parts. Each line occupies two measures of $\frac{6}{8}$ in the transcription, except for the exclamation "O radio!" (O, from your rays), which has only four syllables instead of either seven or six of the rest of the stanza's lines. The short melodic phrases are clearly set off by strokes in the manuscripts, suggesting transcription in either rhythmic mode I or II. The three voices sing the same words at the same time, although only the tenor has text written under it.

Motet: *Amours mi font/En mai/Flos filius eius* 19

1. Montpellier MS (Mo) has a ligature of 3 breves.
2. Mo has *lei.*
3. Mo has *E,* the correct chant note.
4. Mo has *n'oi.*
5. Mo has a ligature of 2 breves.
6. Mo has *deport.*
7. Mo has a ligature of 3 breves+longa.
8. Mo has *m'eves.*
9. Mo has a longa rest.

Reproduced by permission of A-R Editions, Inc., from *The Montpellier Codex,* ed. Hans Tischler, Recent
Researches in the Music of the Middle Ages and Early Renaissance, vols. 4–5. © 1978, A-R Editions, Inc.

TRIPLUM

Amours mi font souffrir peine a tort,	Loving makes me wrongly suffer pain,
Car ma dame, qui m'a mort,	because my lady, who has killed me,
Ne me daigne des maus, qu'ai por li,	does not deign while I am in misery
Douner confort.	to comfort me.
Et si l'ai toz jours mout bien servi,	And if I always served her very well,
N'ainc certes ne li menti.	I certainly never lied to her.
Ains sui toz a son voloir, ne l'en desdi,	That I am entirely at her mercy, I don't deny,
Et ainsi voeil estre adés a son acort.	and so I wish from now on to be in her good graces,
Et toz dis a jointes mains li cri merci,	and every day I clasp my hands and cry for pity,
Pour Diu, qu'ele le deignast avoir de mi!	O Lord, that she grant me mercy.

MOTETUS

En mai, quant rose est florie,	In May, when the rose blooms,
Que j'oi ces oisiaus chanter,	and I hear the birds sing,
Moi covient par druerie	I like by whatever means
Joie demener.	to strive for joy.
C'est la fin, je vuoil amer;	This is it; I want to love.
Et si ne croi mie,	I don't believe
Qu'ele sache ja,	that she yet knows
Don[t] vient li maus d'amer,	where my pains of love come from
Qui m'ocirra.	that will slay me.
Qu'onques en ma vie	Never in my life
D'amors n'ai deport,	have I known love's pleasure,
Mes se je n'ai vostre aïe,	but if I don't have your help,
Vostre amor, vostre confort,	your love, your solace,
Brunete sans ami,	brunette without lover,
Vos m'avés mort.	you will have killed me.

The style of this motet is called *Franconian* after Franco of Cologne, a thirteenth-century composer and theorist who described a notation in which note shapes accurately represented temporal durations and who clarified the rules for consonance and dissonance. All the voices are based on the first rhythmic mode, consisting of a long followed by a breve. In the upper parts both the long and the breve are frequently broken up into shorter notes, a device theorists called *fractio modi* (breaking up of the mode).

A pairing of this tenor with this motetus appears in a clausula in the manuscript Wolfenbüttel 2, so what we have here may be regarded as two compositions in one, a two-part and a three-part motet, and it may be performed either way.

The tenor performs the chant melody of *Flos filius eius* (see example below) twice (measures 1–12 and 13–25), repeating throughout a rhythmic pattern that occupies two measures of the transcription. Since the music of the motetus originated as a clausula duplum, the French text must have been composed after the music. This accounts for the uneven lengths of poetic lines and the irregular rhyme scheme. The triplum's text and melody are more independent, and its textual-musical lines do not match those of the motetus but sometimes overlap. This feature, together with the breaking up of the rhythmic mode, assures constant animation, and helps to avert the stops and starts found in many motets of this period.

Verse, *Virgo Dei Genitrix*, of the responsory *Stirps Jesse* for the feast of the Blessed Virgin Mary (*Processionale monasticum* [Solesmes: Petrus, 1893], p. 186).

The first and last (sixth) notes of the tenor's modal pattern receive the most perfect consonances—namely, the unison, fifth, and octave—but there are exceptions. Dissonances and imperfect consonances fall mainly on the short notes of the mode or on the second halves of the long notes. The tenor's rhythmic pattern cleverly emphasizes the two most characteristic degrees of the chant's Hypodorian mode (II), the final *D* and the reciting tone *F*. The upper parts share the complementary authentic range of Dorian mode (I).

20

PHILIPPE DE VITRY (1291–1361)
Motet from *Roman de Fauvel*

Garrit Gallus / In nova fert / Neuma

Reprinted from Hoppin, *Anthology of Medieval Music*, No. 59, pp. 120–26.

TRIPLUM

Garrit Gallus flendo dolorose
Luget quippe Gallorum concio.
Que satrape traditur dolose,
Ex cubino sedens officio.
Atque vulpes, tamquam vispilio
in Belial vigens astucia
De leonis consensu proprio
Monarchisat, atat angaria
Rursus, ecce. Jacob familia
Pharaone altero fugatur;
Non ut olim lude vestigia
Subintrare potens, lacrimatur.
In deserto fame flagellatur.
Adiutoris carens armatura.
Quamquam clamat, tamen spoliatur,
Continuo forsan moritura.
O miserum exulum vox dura!
O Gallorum garritus doloris,
Cum leonis cecitas obscura
Fraudi paret vulpis proditoris.
Eius fastus sustinens erroris
Insurgito: alias labitur
Et labetur quod habes honoris,
Quod mox in facinis tardis ultoribus itur.

The cock babbles, lamenting sorrowfully,
for the whole assembly of cocks★
mourns because, while serving vigilantly,
it is trickily betrayed by the satrap.
And the fox,† like a grave robber,
thriving with the astuteness of Belial,
rules as a monarch with the consent
of the lion himself.‡ Ah, what slavery!
Lo, once again Jacob's family
is exiled by another Pharaoh.
Not, as formerly, able to escape
to the homeland of Judah, they weep.
Stricken by hunger in the desert,
lacking the help of arms,
although they cry out, they are robbed;
perhaps speedily they will die.
O harsh voice of the wretched exiles;
O sorrowfully babbling of the cocks,
since the dark blindness of the lion
submits to the fraud of the traitorous fox.
You who suffer the arrogance of his misdeeds,
rise up,
or what you have of honor is being or
will be lost, because if avengers are slow
men soon turn to evil doing.

DUPLUM

In nova fert animus mutatas
Dicere formas.
Draco nequam quam olim penitus
Mirabilis crucis potencia
Debellavit Michael inclitus,
Mox Absalon munitus gracia,
Mox Ulixis gaudens facundia,
Mox lupinis dentibus armatus,
Sub Tersitis miles milicia
Rursus vivit in vulpem mutatus,
Cauda cuius, lumine privatus
Leo, vulpe imperante, paret.
Oves suggit pullis saciatus.

Heu! suggere non cessat et aret
Ad nupcias carnibus non caret.
Ve pullis mox, ve ceco leoni!
Coram Christotandem ve draconi.

My heart is set upon speaking of forms
changed into new (bodies).§
The evil dragon that renowned Michael once
utterly defeated by the miraculous power
of the Cross,
now endowed with the grace of Absalom,
now with the cheerful eloquence of Ulysses,
now armed with wolfish teeth
a soldier in the service of Thersites,
lives again changed into a fox
whose tail the lion deprived
of sight obeys, while the fox reigns.
He sucks the blood of sheep and is satiated
with chickens.
Alas, he does not cease sucking and still thirsts;
he does not abstain from meats at the wedding feast.
Woe now to the chickens, woe to the blind lion.
In the presence of Christ, finally, woe to the dragon.

—RICHARD HOPPIN

★Gallus: cock; or Gauls (the French)
†Enguerran de Marigny, chief councillor of the French king
‡Philip IV the Fair
§Ovid *Metamorphoses*, 1,1.

The *Roman de Fauvel* is a satirical poem preserved in a beautifully decorated manuscript dating from 1310–14 (Paris, Bibliothèque nationale, MS fr. 146; see the illumination from this codex reproduced in HWM, p. 104). *Garrit Gallus,* one of thirty-four polyphonic motets in the manuscript, illustrates a unifying technique called isorhythm in which the durational values of the tenor notes are laid out in segments of identical rhythm (*iso* means same).

If we examine the tenor of *Garrit Gallus* we see that the composer divided the melody on *Neuma* into three equal parts (1–25, 26–50, and 51–75) to fit three statements of the rhythmic pattern, or *talea* (a cutting or segment). The melody is then repeated (measures 77–145) for a second *color* (repetition in rhetorical terminology), using identical taleae. This organization may be perceived at a glance in the example that follows:

Garrit Gallus displays yet another level of complexity. The tenor in the original notation was written partly in red ink to warn the singer that the segment in this "colored" notation is in duple meter as opposed to the triple of black notation. In the score (and in the example above) these segments are enclosed in incomplete brackets. The colored segment (measures 7–16 and elsewhere) consists in the transcription of five times two $\frac{6}{8}$ units. On either side are two times three $\frac{6}{8}$ units. Such mixing of duple and triple grouping is one of the novel techniques of the *ars nova* that distinguishes it from the *ars antiqua,* in which triple grouping of durations was preferred. Another distinctive feature of this tenor is that the colored segment is built symmetrically around the dotted whole-note rest in the middle.

As we may often note in isorhythmic motets, there is an audible form almost in conflict with the isorhythmic structure yet subtly influenced by it.

In *Garrit Gallus* the beginnings and ends of poetic lines seem to have little relationship to the beginnings and ends of the tenor's taleae. The two upper parts, however, are clearly coordinated; the duplum always finishes its phrase and rests one measure before the triplum. These points, instead of coinciding with ends of the tenor's taleae, are related to the colored segments, in that the duplum almost always rests at the beginning of a colored segment while the triplum rests at the end. The colored segments also influence the triplum in another significant way: the triplum is isorhythmic above three of them (at measures 32, 57, and 82). The duple-triple opposition consequently emerges as the structural feature that the listener will judge the most important.

roundeau Form (handwritten)

21 GUILLAUME DE MACHAUT (CA. 1300–1377)

Rondeau: *Rose, liz, printemps, verdure*

main melody (ballade style) (cantilena) (handwritten)

Triplum

[Cantus]
1-2.6-7.11-12. Ro - se,   liz,
54 / 16 / 4 - 5. Et tous   les
55 / 17 / 8 - 9. Et quant   tou -

Contratenor

Tenor

prin - temps, ver - du - re,   Fleur,
biens de Na - tu - re,   A
- te cre - a - tu - re   Seur -

bau - me
vez
- mon

Guillaume de Machaut, *Polyphonic Music of the Fourteenth Century,* vol. 3, ed. Leo Schrade (Monaco: Éditions de l'Oiseau-Lyre, 1974), pp. 11–12.

Rose, liz, printemps, verdure,
  Fleur, baume et tres douce odour,
Belle, passes en doucour,
  Et tous les biens de Nature,
  Avez dont je vous aour.
Rose, liz, printemps, verdure,
  Fleur, baume et tres douce odour.

Rose, lily, spring, greenery,
flower, balm, and the sweetest fragrance,
beautiful lady, you surpass in sweetness.
And all the gifts of nature
you possess, for which I adore you.
Rose, lily, spring, greenery,
flower, balm, and the sweetest fragrance.

Et quant toute creature	And, since beyond any creature's
Seurmonte vostre valour,	your virtue excels,
Bien puis dire et par honour:	I can honestly say:
Rose, liz, printemps, verdure,	Rose, lily, spring, greenery,
Fleur, baume et tres douce odour,	flower, balm, and very sweet fragrance,
Belle, passes en doucour.	beautiful lady, you surpass in sweetness.

The rondeau is a form in which the full refrain, heard at the beginning and the end, contains all the music. In *Rose, liz* the first part of the refrain has two lines and closes without finality on *D*, while the second part has one line and closes on the keytone *C*. The first couplet, of two lines, is set to the music of the first part of the refrain; the second couplet, of three lines, uses all the music. The musical form for the 13 lines is A B a A a b A B (capital letters indicate that both the music and the text of the refrain are sung):

Line:	1	2	3	4	5	6(1)	7(2)	8	9	10	11(1)	12(2)	13(3)
Rhyme:	a	b	b	a	b	a	b	a	b	b	a	b	b
Music:	A		B	a		A		a		b	A		B

A and B are linked by having similar final rhymes and musical phrases (compare measures 20–25 and 32–36).

As in Machaut's secular songs in general, the music is constructed around a two-voice framework in which the tenor serves as a slower-moving support to the cantus, the only voice provided with a text (although all of the voices may have been sung). The contratenor, in the same range as the tenor, reinforces or complements it, while the triplum shares the upper octave and exchanges motives with the cantus. A diatonic descending-fourth figure dominates the tenor part and at one point is taken up by the triplum (compare tenor, measures 11–12, and triplum, measures 15–16). Thirds and sixths sweeten the harmony along the way but are suppressed at the final note of poetic lines and caesuras, where Machaut preferred the octave and fifth. What may sound like syncopations are really the effect of hemiola, parts simultaneously organized in duple and triple divisions ($\frac{6}{8}$ and $\frac{3}{4}$ in the transcription).

Characteristic of French fourteenth-century secular music is the long melisma at the beginning of lines and sometimes also in the middle. These melismas, occupying as much as four measures, do not fall on important words, nor even necessarily on accented syllables. They have a formal and decorative function and help convey the mood of the text.

GUILLAUME DE MACHAUT

Mass: Agnus Dei

Edited by Elizabeth Keitel for "Early Musical Masterworks." For translation of text, see p. 17.

Machaut's *Messe de Notre Dame* was one of the earliest polyphonic settings of the Ordinary. At least four more or less complete anonymous cycles preceded it, but Machaut's stands out for its spacious dimensions, its control of consonance and dissonance in a four-part texture, and its carefully planned isorhythmic structures. Although it is not unified, as some later Masses, by a single cantus firmus—each movement is based on a different one—there is a unity of approach and style and a tonal focus on *D* and *F* that hold the movements together.

The Kyrie, Sanctus, Agnus Dei, and Ite, missa est are organized by means of isorhythm, a manner of construction Machaut used in his motets. The Agnus Dei is typical of the isorhythmic movements. The tenor melody is taken from the setting of that text in the plainchant Mass numbered XVII in modern chant books (*Liber usualis*, p. 61), though in a slightly different version. The isorhythmic structure begins at the words "qui tollis"—that is, after the intonation of each Agnus (Agnus III repeats Agnus I). Since the "qui tollis" section of the chant is identical in Agnus I and II, the two statements of this constitute the two colores. The first color (Agnus I) has two taleae, each of twelve notes; the second color (Agnus II) has six taleae, each of four notes. The more frequent cadences at the end of the short taleae of Agnus II set it apart and provide contrast with the longer spans of Agnus I (and its repetition in Agnus III). In addition to the tenor, the triplum and contratenor are also wholly or partly isorhythmic.

The two upper parts enliven the rhythm with almost constant syncopation. A characteristic motive outlining a tritone is heard a number of times (measures 2, 5, and 25, and in ornamented form in 19), also in other movements of the Mass.

The occasion for which the work was written is not known, despite a persistent but undocumented hunch that it was for the coronation of the French King Charles V in 1364; whatever the occasion, it must have been one of unusual solemnity and magnificence. On the basis of comparison with datable songs, it seems to be from the early 1360s.

Jacopo da Bologna (14th century)

Madrigal: *Fenice fù*

αFenice fù e vissi pura e morbida,
  Et or son trasmutat' in una tortora,
  Che volo con amor per le belle ortora
αArbor[e] secho [mai] n'aqua torbida,

A phoenix was I who lived pure and tender
and now am transformed into a turtle-dove
that flies with love through the beautiful orchards, [and]
the dry woods [but] never in muddy waters.

Nino Pirrotta, ed. *The Collected Works of Jacobo da Bologna and Vincenzo da Rimini* (American Institute of Musicology, 1963), p. 6.

No' me deleta may per questo dubito,	It gives me no pleasure because of this doubt.
Va ne l'astate l'inverno viene subito.	Go in the summer; winter comes quickly.
Tal vissi e tal me vivo e posso scrivere	So I lived and so I live and can write,
C'ha donna non è più chè honesta vivere.	which, for a woman, is no more than to live honestly.

The poem set here has the form typical of the fourteenth-century madrigal: two three-line stanzas followed by a two-line ritornello. Thus the music of the stanza is heard twice, and the ritornello once. The two voices have the same text, and both parts were meant to be sung. In two places (measures 7–9, 24–25) they are in imitation, and in two short passages (measures 9, 16) they indulge in a hocket-like alternation. Otherwise the upper voice is the more florid one, having extended mellifluous runs on the last accented syllable of each line.

Jacopo's birth and death dates are not known, but between 1346 and 1349 and again in the 1350s his service to the ruling family of Milan, the Visconti, and in between at the court of Mastino II and Alberto della Scala of Verona, is well documented. *Fenice fù* is probably one of his last compositions.

FRANCESCO LANDINI (CA. 1327–1397)

Ballata: *Non avrà ma' pietà*

Ballade style

Leo Schrade, ed. *Polyphonic Music of the Fourteenth Century*, 4 (Paris: Éditions de l'Oiseau-Lyre, 1958), pp. 144–45.

A Non avrà ma' pietà questa mia donna,
  Se tu non faj, amore,
  Ch'ella sie certa del mio grande ardore.
b S'ella sapesse quanta pena i' porto
A Per onestà celata nella mente
b Sol per la sua bellecça, che conforto
α D'altro non prende l'anima dolente,
α Forse da lej sarebbono in me spente
  Le fiamme che la pare
  Di giorno in giorno acrescono'l dolore.

(back to A)

She will never have mercy, this lady of mine,
if you do not see to it, love,
that she is certain of my great ardor.
If she knew how much pain I bear—
for honesty's sake concealed in my mind—
only for her beauty, other than which
nothing gives comfort to a grieving soul,
perhaps by her would be extinguished in me
the flames which seem to arouse in
her from day to day more pain.

—B. D'ALESSIO DONATI

This ballata is typical of the form adopted by Francesco Landini. A two-line refrain (*ripresa*) is sung both before and after a six-line stanza. The first two pairs of lines in the stanza, which were called *piedi*, have their own musical phrase, while the last pair, the *volta*, uses the same music as the refrain. The form may be represented as follows:

Poetic form:	ripresa			stanza (2 piedi + volta)						ripresa		
Poetic lines:	1	2	3	4	5	6	7	8	9	10	1	2	3
Music:	A			b		b		a			A		

Having a melisma on the first as well as the penultimate syllable of a line is characteristic of the Italian style. The end of every line, and often of the first word and of the caesura, is marked by a cadence, usually of the type that has become known as the *Landini cadence*, in which the movement from a major sixth to an octave is ornamented by a lower neighbor leaping up a third in the upper part (see measures 3–4, 5–6, 10–11). Sometimes both the voices that rise to the final chord do so by semitone motion, either written or by musica ficta (feigned or fictitious music)—so called because it is not in the governing mode or scale (*musica vera*), as in measures 3–4—and this form of the cadence is known as the *double leading-tone cadence*.

The use of the open (*verto*) and closed (*chiuso*) endings in the two *piedi*, represented in the transcription by the first and second endings at measure 34, may be traced to the influence of the French virelai.

One of the charms of Landini's music, in addition to the graceful vocal melody, is the sweetness of its harmonies. Gone are the parallel seconds and sevenths that abounded in the thirteenth century, and there are few parallel fifths and octaves. Sonorities containing both the intervals of the third and fifth or of the third and sixth are plentiful, though they are not used to start or end a section or piece.

25 Baude Cordier (late 14th or early 15th century)

Rondeau: *Belle, bonne, sage*

Transcribed by Gilbert Reaney in *Early Fifteenth-Century Music* (American Institute of Musicology, 1955), pp. 9–10.

cy   que   l'an   se re - nou - - ne vel - - - -
pli,   ma   doul - ce   da - moy - - sel
que   vous e - stes seu - le   cel

le, 3-4 15-16. vous fais   le   don d'u - ne chan   son   nou
le,
le 11-12.   qui fa - mea - vés que cha - - scun vous ap-

- vel - - - - - - le || de - dans mon
- pel - - - - - - le: || flour de beau-

cuer   qui   a vous se - - pre - sen - - - - -
té   sur tou - tes ex - - cel - len - - - -

Belle, bonne, sage, plaisante et gente,
A ce jour cy que l'an se renouvelle
Vous fais le don d'une chanson nouvelle
Dedens mon coeur qui a vous se presente.

De recevoir ce don ne soyes lente,
Je vous suppli, ma douce demoiselle.
Belle bonne sage plaisante et gente,
A ce jour cy que l'an se renouvelle.

Car tant vous aim qu'ailleurs n'aymon entente,
Et sy scay que vous estes seule celle
Qui fame aves que chascun vous appelle:
Flour de beaute sur toutes excellente.

Belle bonne sage plaisante et gente,
A ce jour cy que l'an se renouvelle
Vous fais le don d'une chanson nouvelle
Dedens mon coeur qui a vous se presente.

Fair lady, good, wise, pleasant, and nice,
on this day when the year is renewed
I make a gift of a new song
within my heart which presents itself to you.

Be not slow in accepting this gift,
I beg you, my sweet damsel.
Fair lady, good, wise, pleasant, and nice,
on this day when the year is renewed.

I love you so much that I have lost my senses,
and I know that you alone
have the fame that everyone calls you
flower of beauty surpassing all.

Fair lady, good, wise, pleasant, and nice,
on this day when the year is renewed
I make a gift of a new song
within my heart which presents itself to you.

Baude Cordier's rondeau, *Belle, bonne, sage*, participates half-seriously in the intellectual play of the *ars subtilior* (subtler art) of the late fourteenth century. But this song is not much more subtle in its music than in its heart-shaped graphic presentation. If there is complexity in the music, it lies in the three levels of hemiola. When the composer departed from the regular fast triple division to a slow triple as in the contratenor at measures 7–11 (from $\frac{3}{4}$ to $\frac{3}{2}$ in the transcription), he indicated this with red notes (see the color illustration in HWM, p. 120). He also used red notes when he wanted triple division against the duple values of the $\frac{3}{2}$ sections (measure 8) or when he wanted a duple division in the cantus against the contratenor's $\frac{3}{4}$ (measures 11–12). In the text, in the line "within my heart which presents itself to you," the word "heart" is replaced with a red heart, and, of course, the entire piece is notated in the shape of a heart. An unusual feature of this chanson is the anticipation by the contratenor and tenor of the opening melody of the voice.

John Dunstable (ca. 1390–1453)

Motet: *Quam pulchra es*

Quam pul-cra es et quam de-co-ra, ca-ris-si-ma in de-li -

Quam pul-cra es et quam de-co-ra, ca-ris-si-ma in de-li -

Quam pul-cra es et quam de-co-ra, ca-ris-si-ma in de-li -

- ci - is. Sta-tu-ra tu - a as-si-mi-la-ta est pal -

- ci - is. Sta-tu-ra tu - a as - si-mi-la-ta est pal -

- ci - is. Sta-tu-ra tu - a as - si-mi-la-ta est pal -

me, et u-be-ra tu-a bo-tris. Ca-put tu-um ut Car - me -

me, et u-be-ra tu-a bo-tris. Ca-put tu - um ut Car - me -

me, et u-be-ra tu-a bo-tris. Ca-put tu-um ut Car - me -

lus, col-lum tu-um si-cut tur - ris e - bur - ne -

lus, col-lum tu-um si-cut tur - ris e - bur - ne -

lus, col - lum tu-um si-cut tur - ris e - bur - ne -

Quam pulchra es et quam decora,
  carissima in deliciis.
Statuta tua assimilata est palme,
  et ubera tua botris.
Caput tuum ut Carmelus,
  collum tuum sicut turris eburnea.
Veni, dilecte mi,
egrediamur in agrum,
et videamus si flores fructus parturierunt
  si floruerunt mala Punica.
Ibi dabo tibi ubera mea.
Alleluia.

—The Song of Solomon 7:6–12

How fair and pleasant you are,
  O loved one in delights.
You are stately as a palm tree,
  and your breasts are like its clusters.
Your head crowns you like Carmel;
  your neck is like an ivory tower.
Come, my beloved,
let us go forth into the fields,
and see whether the grape blossoms have opened
  and the pomegranates are in bloom.
There I will give you my love.
Alleluia.

—Adapted from the Revised Standard Version of the Bible

Dunstable wrote numerous settings of antiphons, hymns, and other liturgical or biblical texts for a three-part ensemble, most of them based on chant melodies. This antiphon, however, is freely composed.

The three voices, similar in character and of nearly equal importance, move mostly in the same rhythm and usually pronounce the same syllables together. The musical texture resembles that of the conductus, and the short melisma at the end of the word "alleluia" conforms with the ornamented conductus style.

The composer, unfettered by a cantus firmus or an isorhythmic scheme, freely determined the form of the music, guided only by the text. Dunstable divided the piece into two sections. Section one (measures 1–38) comprises in shortened form verses 6, 7, 5, 4, and 11 of Chapter 7 of The Song of Solomon; section two, beginning with "et videamus," draws on verse 12, with an added "alleluia." The longer first section is punctuated near the end by sustained notes on the word "veni" (come); its pattern of subdivision is 9 + 9 + 11 + 8 measures, with cadences on C, C, D, and G. The second section subdivides symmetrically into 4 + 3 + 6 + 3 + 4 measures, with cadences on F, D, C, D, and C. The musical subdivisions of the first section correspond to the division of the text into verses; those of section two are less distinct, just as the subdivisions of the text are less clearly marked than in section one, but the "alleluia" is definitely set off by its melisma and the livelier melodic and harmonic rhythm approaching the final cadence.

Not only is the musical form determined by the text, many phrases are molded to the rhythm of the words—for example, in the declamation of "statuta tua assimilata est," "mala Punica," and "ibi dabo tibi." Other notable details are: the frequent use of melodic thirds in the topmost voice, the occasional outlining of a triad in the melody (for example, in measures 43, 46, 55), and the passages of fauxbourdon, particularly at the approach to a cadence (as in measures 12–15, 32–34, 44–45, and 52–54).

27 Carol: *Salve, sancta parens*

John Stevens, ed. *Mediaeval Carols.* Musica Britannica 4 (London: Stainer & Bell, 1952), p. 71. Reprinted by permission.

Salve, sancta parens,	Hail, holy parent,
Enixa puerpera Regem.	from a woman in labor issued a King.
Salve, porta paradisi,	Hail, gate of paradise,
Felix atque fixa,	happy and firm,
Stella fulgens in sublimi	start shining on high
Sidus enixa.	from which a constellation sprang.

The carol, originally a monophonic dance song with alternating solo and choral portions, had by the fifteenth century become stylized as a setting in two or three (sometimes four) parts. The text was a religious poem in popular style. The carol consisted of a number of stanzas all sung to the same music, and a *burden* (a refrain with its own musical phrase), which was sung at the beginning and then repeated after each stanza.

In this carol, the music for the stanza, marked *verse*, is in free two-part counterpoint. The burden is sung twice: the first time the two parts move mostly in parallel sixths; the second time a middle voice largely parallels the top voice at a fourth below while making a third with the lowest. At the ends of poetic lines, the voices move out from parallel sixths and thirds to octaves and fifths. Measures 16 to 19 illustrate the technique of making such a cadence. This piece reflects the English improvised practice of discant, which tolerated longer successions of parallel sixths (unmediated by perfect consonances) than Continental discant and tended to put the chant or traditional melody in the top voice.

28 GUILLAUME DUFAY (CA. 1400–1474)

Ballade: *Resvellies vous et faites chiere lye*

Dufay, *Opera omnia*, ed. Heinrich Besseler, vol. 6 (American Institute of Musicology, 1964), pp. 25–26.

10

A Resvellies vous et faites chiere lye
   Tout amoureux qui gentilesse ames
A Esbates vous, fuyes merancolye,
   De bien servir point ne soyes hodés
B Car au jour d'ui sera li espousés,
   Par grant honneur et noble seignourie;
   Ce vous convient ung chascum faire feste,
   Pour bien grignier la belle compagnye;
C Charle gentil, c'on dit de Maleteste.

   Il a dame belle et bonne choysie,
   Dont il sera grandement honnourés;
   Car elle vient de tres noble lignie
   Et de barons qui sont mult renommés.
   Son propre nom est Victoire clamés;
   De la colonne vient sa progenie.
   C'est bien rayson qu'a vascule requeste
   De cette dame mainne bonne vie.
   Charle gentil, c'on dit de Maleteste.

Awake and be merry,
lovers all who love gentleness;
frolic and flee melancholy.
Tire not of serving yourself well,
for today will be the nuptials,
with great honor and noble lordship,
and it behooves you, everyone, to celebrate
and join the happy company.
Noble *Charles*, who is named *Malatesta*.

He has chosen a lady, fair and good,
by whom he will be greatly honored,
for she comes from a very noble lineage
of barons who are much renowned.
Her name is *Victoria*,
and she descends from the *Collonas*.
It is right, therefore, that his appeal be heard
to live honestly with this lady.
Noble *Charles*, who is named *Malatesta*.

"Awake and be merry," this ballade tells lovers. It was written for the marriage of Carlo Malatesta and Vittoria Colonna, niece of Pope Martin V, in 1423, when Dufay was serving the ruling family of Rimini and Pesaro. The acclamation "noble Charles," addressed to the bridegroom, is set in block chords with fermatas, while the family name Malatesta gives rise to an orgy of rapid triplets in the superius. The florid treatment at the ends of other lines follows the refined ballade tradition. These passages, with their rapid, angular figurations, seem suited more to instrumental than vocal performance, yet they could easily have been carried off by a trained singer.

This work provides a good example of the treble-dominated style; the two lower parts are less suited to vocal performance, though the players probably joined the soloist in singing "Charle gentil," a passage in the sources where all three parts have text.

The standard AAB musical form of the ballade is heard twice, once for each stanza. The last line of each stanza is a refrain. Hemiola and syncopations abound in both the A and B sections, but the B section is more stately and less agitated.

GUILLAUME DUFAY

Hymn: *Conditor alme siderum*

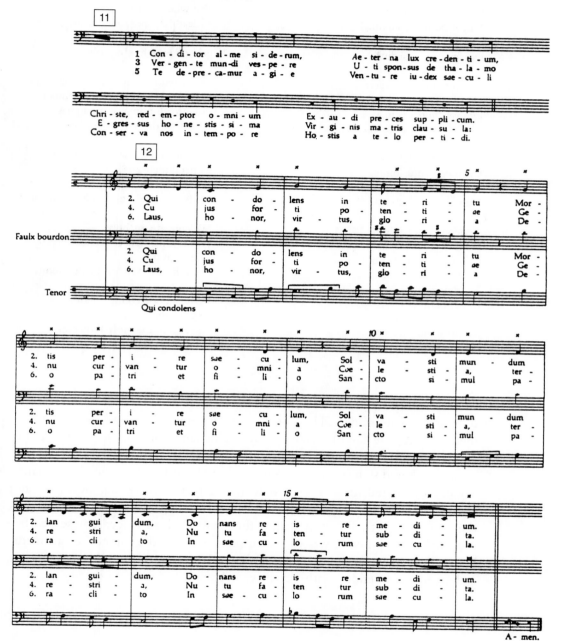

Chant from *Antiphonale*, Appendix, pp. 11–12. Dufay, *Opera omnia*, ed. Heinrich Besseler, vol. 5 (American Institute of Musicology, 1964), p. 39.

Conditor alme siderum,	Bountiful creator of the stars,
Aeterna lux credentium,	eternal light of believers,
Christe redemptor omnium	Christ, redeemer of all,
Exaudi preces supplicum.	hear the prayers of the supplicants.
Qui condolens interitu	You who suffer the ruin
Mortis perire saeculum,	of death, the perishing of the race,
Solvasti mundum languidum,	who saved the sick world,
Donans reis remedium:	bringing the healing balm.
Vergente mundi vespere	As the world turns toward evening,
Uti sponsus de thalamo,	the bridegroom from his chamber
Egressus honestissima	issues forth from the most chaste
Virginis matris clausula.	cloister of the Virgin mother.
Cujus forti potentiae	You, before whose mighty power
Genu curvantur omnia	all bend their knees,
Coelestia, terrestria,	celestial, terrestrial,
Nutu fatentur subdita.	confessing subjection to his command.
Te deprecamur agie	We entreat you, holy
Venture judex saeculi	judge of the days to come,
Conserva nos in tempore	save us in time
Hostis a telo perfidi.	from the weapons of the perfidious.
Laus, honor, virtus, gloria	Praise, honor, courage, glory,
Deo patri, et filio,	to God, the Father, and Son,
Sancto simul paraclito	and also to the Holy Protector,
in saeculorum saecula.	time everlasting, amen.

In performing a plainchant hymn, it was customary for a chorus and soloists to sing alternate stanzas. The poetry was rhymed and followed an accentual meter—here, the iambic—which the plainchant notation reflected in the succession of breve-long neumes. Dufay wrote polyphonic versions for the even-numbered stanzas in the manner of fauxbourdon. He placed the chant, slightly decorated, in the top voice (the asterisks mark the notes of the chant). Against this voice he wrote a part that began an octave lower and then moved mostly in sixths against the chant. A third voice, represented by the smaller note-heads, was expected to be sung at the interval of a fourth below the chant, producing a succession of third-sixth sonorities, except at cadences, which ended with an octave between the outer voices.

GUILLAUME DUFAY

Se la face ay pale

30

a) Ballade

Se la face ay pale,
La cause est amer,
Et tant m'est amer
Amer, qu'en la mer
Me voudroye voir;
Or, scet bien de voir
La belle a qui suis
Que nul bien avoir
Sans elle ne puis.

If my face is pale,
the cause is love,
and it is so bitter for me
to love, that in the sea
I would throw myself.
Then would she see—
the fair lady to whom I belong—
that no joy can I have
without her.

Dufay, *Opera omnia*, ed. Heinrich Besseler (American Institute of Musicology, 1951–66), 6:36 (ballade); 3:5–13 (Mass).

b) *Missa Se la face ay pale*: Gloria

For the text of the Gloria, see NAWM 3.

For this Mass, perhaps written for a special occasion at the court of Savoy in
the 1450s, Dufay used the tenor of his own ballade, *Se la face ay pale*
(NAWM 30a), composed in the 1430s, as a cantus firmus. The chanson, of
which only the first of three stanzas is given here, is not in the usual ballade
form—A A B—but is through-composed.

In the Mass, Dufay used the ballade's tenor melody as a cantus firmus, applying mensural proportions so that it is heard at different speeds in the several movements or sections. In the Kyrie, Sanctus, and Agnus the value of each note of the ballade is doubled. In the Gloria and in the Credo the cantus firmus is heard three times, first at triple the normal note values, then with doubled note values, and finally at normal note values, so that the melody becomes easily recognizable only when it is heard at its normal pace this third time. As a result, each measure of the tenor corresponds to three measures of the other parts in measures 19–118; to two measures of the other parts in measures 125–158; and to one measure in measures 165–198. Thus the calculated restatement of the tune imposes on the Gloria a form that is further marked by preceding each entrance of the cantus firmus with a duet. The speeding up of the tenor's cantus firmus and the imitation of some of its motives in the other parts contribute to the excitement of the closing Amen.

More immediately evident to the listener than the unity achieved by the threefold statement of the chanson melody in the tenor is the diverse character of the several voices. Each is an independent layer having its own melodic and rhythmic logic and function. The top two voices—the superius and the contratenor altus—have soft melodious contours and occasionally exchange motives, while the contratenor bassus, more angular though still vocal, provides a harmonic foundation.

The most obvious level of temporal organization is the perfect tempus, represented in the transcription by the $\frac{3}{2}$ measures. Each of the three beats within this tempus is divided into two (minor prolation). A broader triple organization is evident in the tenor's perfect modus consisting of three tempora, or three of the modern measures. Interrupting this pattern are an instance of hemiola in measures 19–20 between the superius–contratenor altus and the tenor bassus, and shifts in meter at measures 26, 34, and 36 in the altus, from the prevailing $\frac{3}{2}$ to a compound duple $\frac{6}{4}$.

Besides the repetitions of the ballade tune throughout the Mass, another unifying feature is the so-called *head motive*, or *motto*. Each principal division of a movement begins in the uppermost voice with the motive that in the Gloria is set to the words "Et in terra pax." The motive is alluded to also within movements, as in the Gloria at measures 40, 88, 119, 165, and 184.

Although the ballade is clearly centered on *C*, and many of the internal cadences in the Mass movement also close on this tonality, Dufay left himself free to center the Mass on *F* by putting the tune in the tenor. The choice of *F* as the center permitted greater tonal variety, since *C* remains a focus for some of the subdivisions of the work.

Consonance and dissonance are also under rational control. The stronger lingering dissonances are properly resolved suspensions, as at measures 33, 36, 72, and 81, while other dissonances, mainly between beats, pass quickly. Otherwise, the composer obviously strove to include as many thirds and sixths—along with octaves, fifths, and fourths—among the parts as possible, producing many triads (to use modern terminology) on the beats of the tempus.

31 JOHANNES OCKEGHEM (CA. 1420–1497)
Chanson: *D'ung aultre amer*

D'ung aultre amer mon cueur s'abesseroit,
Il ne fault pas penser que je l'estrange,

Ne que pour rien de ce propos me change.
Car mon honneur en appetisseroit.

Je l'aime tant que jamais ne seroit
Possible a moy d'en consentir l'echange.
D'ung aultre amer . . . (etc.)

To love another my heart would be debased.
It should not be thought that I estrange myself
    from him,
or that anything would bend me from this resolve,
because my honor would be in jeopardy.

I love him so much that never would it be
possible for me to consent to an exchange.
To love another . . . (etc.)

Reprinted by permission of Koninklijke Vereniging voor Nederlandse Muziek geschiedenis, Utrecht, The Netherlands, from *Van Ockeghem tot Sweelinck*, Albert Smijers, ed. (1952), II, 12.

La mort, par Dieu, avant me defferoit,	Death, by God, would sooner unlock me
Qu'en mon vivant j'acointasse ung estrange.	than that in my lifetime I should know a stranger.
Ne cuide nul qu'a cela je me renge,	Think not that I would adapt myself to this.
Ma loyaulté trop fort se mesferoit.	My fidelity would be too much damaged.
D'ung aultre amer . . . (etc.)	To love another . . . (etc.)

This piece is a rondeau, holding to the medieval form:

AB   four refrain lines
a   two new lines of text sung to the first half of the
       refrain's music
A   the first two lines of the refrain with their music
ab   a new four-line stanza sung to the refrain's music
AB   return of the full refrain's text and music

The melody appears in the top voice, which is also the only one to bear a text in the sources, leading scholars to suggest that the other parts would have been played on instruments. The setting is mainly syllabic except for the accented syllable of the last word, which has a flowing melisma. The composer took great care to assure that a complete triad is heard whenever possible within the three-voice texture. Josquin quoted the first line of the text and music in his motet *Tu solus, qui facis mirabilia* (NAWM 33).

32 JOSQUIN DES PREZ (CA. 1440–1521)
Mille regretz — *1000 regrets music printed*

a) Chanson

First published in a lute arrangement by Hans Newsidler, *Ein New geordnet Künstlich Lautenbuch* (Nuremberg, 1536). Reprinted by permission of the publishers from *The Chanson and Madrigal,* ed. James Haar. Cambridge, Mass.; Harvard University Press, © 1968 by the President and Fellows of Harvard College.

Mille regretz de vous habandonner
Et d'eslonger vostre fache amoureuse,
Jay si grand dueil et paine douloureuse,
Quon me verra brief mes jours definer.

A thousand regrets at deserting you
and leaving behind your loving face.
I feel so much sadness and such painful distress,
that it seems to me my days will soon dwindle away.

b) Arrangement for vihuela by Luis de Narváez (ca. 1500–after ca. 1555)

Narváez, *Los seys libros del Delphin de música de cifras para vihuela* (Valladolid, 1538). In this source the song is named "La cancion del Emperador," and may have been among "aucunes chanssons nouvelles" delivered by Josquin to Charles V in September 1520. See *Die Musik in Geschichte und Gegenwart*, vii, 197. Edited by Geneviève Thibault in "Instrumental Transcriptions of Josquin's French Chansons," in *Josquin des Prez*, ed. Edward E. Lowinsky (London: Oxford University Press, 1976), pp. 464–66.

In this chanson every voice is essential, the treble-dominated style having been abandoned. That all the voices were meant to be sung is most evident when a pair of voices answers another pair, as at the words "et paine douloureuse" (measures 19–24), or when one voice imitates another, as the altus imitates the cantus (measures 24–30), or when the entire choir syllabically declaims the same half-line three times (measures 34–38). The sad mood of the text is expressed through the choice of Mode 3 on *E*, which favors cadences on the minor triad on *A* (as at measures 22, 24, 32) and a plagal cadence at the end. The pervasive motive of the descending fourth, most of all in the top voice, contributes to the mournful feeling.

This chanson, perhaps written for Charles V in 1520, was one of Josquin's last and was to become one of the most popular after his death. It was reworked in a Mass by Morales and arranged for vihuela by Luis de Narváez in his *Los seys libros del Delphin* of 1538. The arranger has effectively preserved four-voice texture but has introduced runs and turns of shorter notes, called "diminutions" or "divisions," which enliven the rhythm and often add weight to the downbeats. Narváez also tended to expand the minor sixth to a major sixth by sharping the upper note, as in measures 4, 5, 9, and elsewhere, a license of musica ficta that singers of the time may not have taken as freely.

JOSQUIN DES PREZ

Motet: *Tu solus, qui facis mirabilia*

early motet homorhythmic & homophonic

Motetti di passione (Venice, 1503), ed. George Hunter in New York Pro Musica Series, No. 36 (New York and London: Associated Music Publishers, 1973), pp. 3–12.

[Secunda pars]

Tu solus, qui facis mirabilia;	You only, who do wonders,
Tu solus Creator, qui creasti nos;	You, the only Creator, who created us,
Tu solus Redemptor, qui redemisti nos	You only are the Redeemer, who redeemed us
sanguine tuo pretiosissimo.	with Your most precious blood.
Ad te solum confugimus,	In You alone we seek refuge,
In te solum confidimus,	in You alone we place our trust,
Nec alium adoramus, Jesu Christe.	and no other do we adore, Jesus Christ.
Ad te preces effundimus,	To You we offer our prayers,
Exaudi quod supplicamus,	hear what we beg of You,
Et concede quod petimus,	and grant what we request,
Rex benigne!	benign King.
D'ung aultre amer, nobis esset fallacia;	To love another would be deceitful:
D'ung aultre amer, magna esset stultitia et peccatum.	To love another would be great folly and sin.
Audi nostra suspiria,	Hear our sighs,
Reple nos tua gratia, O Rex regum:	fill us with Your grace, O King of kings,
Ut ad tua servitia sistamus cum laetitia in aeternum.	that we may remain in Your service with joy forever.

This motet, which apparently dates from Josquin's early years, may be modeled in part on the kind of harmony Josquin heard in Italian psalm singing and popular music. Sections of four-part declamatory homorhythmic music alternate with episodes in which pairs of voices imitate each other. The homophonic sections resemble *falsobordone,* a technique used in Italy and Spain to harmonize recitation tones in singing psalms, Magnificats, and Lamentations in four parts. Each simultaneity contains both the third and the fifth to the bass, resulting in what we would now call a series of root-position chords. This kind of harmony is also found in the carnival songs and frottole of the period (see NAWM 36). In some manuscripts of this piece certain successions of such harmonies have fermatas above them, indicating flexible durations. The division of the choir into voice pairs at the words "Ad te solum confugimus, in te solum confidimus" is an exceptionally fine use of this common device, suggested here naturally by the parallelism of the words.

The *secunda pars* (second part) of the motet opens with a quotation of Ockeghem's chanson *D'ung aultre amer* (NAWM 31), partly explainable by the fact that the motet *Tu solus* appears as a substitute for the *Benedictus* in Josquin's Mass *D'ung aultre amer.* Such substitutions were practiced particularly in Milan, where Josquin worked until about 1505. The chanson phrase combines with the Latin text to underscore the sentiment "To love another [than Christ] would be deceitful"—D'ung aultre amer nobis esset *fallacia.* The cryptic reference would have both amused and needled the singers and worshipers of a princely chapel (such as that of Josquin's employer Duke Galeazzo Maria Sforza), who were familiar with the French chanson repertory.

JOSQUIN DES PREZ
Motet: *De profundis clamavi ad te*

Handwritten annotations: used repetition sections to set off style, large duet style, voices independent of each other, very little chordal texture, Psalm, duple meter, late motet, drive to cadence, chordal style, modal

Josquin Desprez, *Werken*, ed. A. Smijers et al (Amsterdam, 1921–), *Motetten*, deel 3, aflevering 35, pp. 20–25.

For the text and translation of Psalm 129, see NAWM 4i.

SECUNDA PARS

This motet is believed to date from the last twenty years of Josquin's life. The close attention the composer paid to the form, rhythm, accentuation, and meaning of the text makes it stand out among his late works.

The construction of the musical periods clearly reflects the double versicles of the psalm. The strongest cadences mark the ending of each verse and the beginning of the next, as at measures 23 (plagal cadence), 40–41, 61–62, 80 (the only Phrygian cadence), 96 (plagal cadence), 111, 122, 133, and 142 (plagal cadence). The prima pars ends on A, the reciting tone of Mode 4 (Hypophrygian), while the *secunda pars* ends on its final, *E*. This is confirmed as the governing mode of the piece by the plagal range of the tenor and superius, which traditionally provided the framework, and the complementary authentic ranges of the bass and alto.

Josquin seized upon the rhythms of certain words to give speechlike vitality to a number of passages—for example, at "propitiatio est" and "et omnibus iniquitatibus." In these instances and throughout the motet he placed the accented syllables on downbeats, syncopated beats, or on notes of relatively longer duration.

Josquin captured the spirit of the whole psalm in the opening line of the superius. It traces the "Dorian" species of fifth (like our A minor), leaping down a fifth for the word "profundis" and reaching up to the minor sixth above for "clamavi," a perfect image of a soul in despair crying for help, straining to be heard. The other voices imitate the first five pitches and durations exactly.

Indeed, the device of imitation pervades the texture. Each new versicle of text receives its own subject, often stated and imitated in paired voices. The moments of simultaneous declamation are few but carefully chosen: "exaudi vocem meam" (hear my voice, measures 20–24), and "sustinui te, Domine" (I have supported Thee, Lord, measures 76–81).

35 HEINRICH ISAAC (CA. 1450–1517)
Lied: *Innsbruck, ich muss dich lassen*

[handwritten: I must leave you]

[handwritten: Style blends Italian, French, Burgundian, & another]

[handwritten: Chordal texture]

[handwritten: Famous works Choralis Constantinus   melody in Soprano]

G. Forster, *Ein ausszug guter und newer teutscher Liedlein* (Nurenberg, 1539). Noah Greenberg and Paul Maynard, *An Anthology of Early Renaissance Music* (New York, 1975), pp. 181–84.

Innsbruck, ich muss dich lassen,
ich fahr dahin mein Strassen,
in fremde Land dahin.
Mein Freud is mir genommen,
die ich nit weiss bekommen,
wo ich im Elend bin.

Gross Leid muss ich jetzt tragen,
das ich allein tu klagen
dem liebsten Buhlen mein.
Ach Lieb, nun lass mich Armen
im Herzen dein erbarmen,
dass ich muss dannen sein.

Mein Trost ob allen Weiben,
dein tu ich ewig bleiben,
stet treu, der Ehren fromm.
Nun muss dich Gott bewahren,
in aller Tugend sparen,
bis dass ich wiederkomm.

Innsbruck, I must leave you
I am going on my way
into a foreign land.
My joy is taken from me,
I know not how to regain it,
while in such misery.

I must now endure great pain
which I confide only
to my dearest love.
O beloved, find pity
in your heart for me,
that I must part from you.

My comfort above all other women,
I shall always be yours,
forever faithful in honor true.
May the good Lord protect you
and keep you in your virtue
for me, till I return.
                    —N. GREENBERG and P. MAYNARD

The polyphonic lied was usually an arrangement of a folk or popular song for four voices, analogous to some of the French chansons. The tune may be in the tenor or treble part and it may or may not use imitation. In the present arrangement, the melody is in the soprano, and, except for some pseudo-imitative entries at the beginning, the other parts harmonize the soprano. A cadence on either *C* or *F* formed with a suspension ends each phrase, followed by a rest, as in the Italian part-songs. This homophonic style looks forward to the texture adopted in the chorale settings arranged for congregational singing. In fact, the melody of this perennial favorite was later adapted to sacred words and became widely known as the chorale *O Welt, ich muss dich lassen* (O world, I now must leave thee).

MARCO CARA (CA. 1470–CA. 1525)

Frottola: *Io non compro più speranza*

Note values halved. Notes in the lute part with dots under them are played with an upward stroke. Bars through the lute staves are original. Those between the voice part and lute accompaniment are added by the present editor to show the true metrical organization. Franciscus Bossinensis, ed., *Tenori e contrabassi intabulati col sopran in canto figurato per cantar e somar col lauto, libro primo* (Venice, 1509). Benvenuto Disertori, ed., *Le Frottole per canto e liuto intabulate da Franciscus Bossinensis* (Milan: Ricordi, 1964), pp. 390–91. Copyright by CASA RICORDI-BMG RICORDI S.p.A., Milan. Reprinted by permission.

Io non compro più speranza
Ché gli è falsa mercancia
A dar sol attendo via
Quella poca che m'avanza.
Io non compro più speranza
Ché gli è falsa mercancia.

35 Cara un tempo la comprai,
Hor la vendo a bon mercato
E consiglio ben che mai
Non ne compri un sventurato
Ma più presto nel suo stato
Se ne resti con costanza.

36 Io non . . .

37 El sperare è come el sogno
Che per più riesce in nulla,
El sperar è proprio il bisogno
De chi al vento si trastulla,
El sperare sovente anulla
Chi continua la sua danza.

38 Io non . . .

I'll buy no more hope,
which is fake goods;
I can't wait to give away
the little that I have left,
I'll buy no more hope,
which is fake goods.

Once I bought it dear;
now I sell it cheap;
and I would advise that never
should the wretched buy it;
rather let them in their condition
remain in constancy.

I'll buy . . .

To hope is like a dream
that mostly results in nothing,
and hoping is the craving need
of him who plays with the wind.
Hoping often annihilates
the one who continues its dance.

I'll buy . . .

This lighthearted complaint of a disappointed lover appeared in Petrucci's first book of frottole (Venice, 1504). The barring in four beats of the lute tablature obscures the dance rhythm of six beats to the measure, as marked off by the bars inserted between the voice and the lute parts. These six beats are organized now in duple groups, now in triple, producing the hemiola so characteristic of the canzonets popular throughout the century and later adopted in seventeenth-century monody. The harmonization consists almost entirely of root chords, a style of harmony that was to have a far-reaching effect on music produced in Italy in the sixteenth century by both native composers and foreigners.

Although the term "frottola" is applied to musical settings of various types of popular poetry, this song manifests the poetic and musical form of the frottola proper, also called *barzelletta*. The poem consists of a four-line *ripresa*, whose first two lines return as a refrain, and a six-line *stanza*, consisting of two two-line *piedi* (literally, feet) and a two-line *volta* (a turning back). The music is coordinated with this poetic structure through the following scheme:

Music mm.	Poetic lines	Rhyme	Poetic form
1–3	Io non compro più speranza	a	
4–6	Ché gli è falsa mercancia	b	⎤—Ripresa
7–9	A dar sol attendo via	b	⎦
10–12	Quella poca che m'avanza.	a	
13–15	Io non compro più speranza	a	⎤—Refrain
16–27	Ché gli è falsa mercancia.	b	⎦
	Stanza 1		
1–3	Cara un tempo la comprai	c	⎤—Piede
4–6	Hor la vendo a bon mercato	d	⎦
1–3	E consiglio ben che mai	c	⎤—Piede
4–6	Non ne compri un sventurato	d	⎦
7–9	Ma più presto nel suo stato	d	⎤—Volta
10–12	Se ne resti con costanza.	a	⎦
13–15	Io non compro più speranza	a	⎤—Refrain
16–27	Ché gli è falsa mercancia.	b	⎦

37 JACOB ARCADELT (CA. 1505–1568)

Madrigal: *Ahime, dov'è 'l bel viso*

Values halved. *Il primo libro di Madrigali d'Archadelt a quatro con nuova gionta impressi* (Venice, 1539); first edition lost but probably from 1538). Arcadelt, *Opera omnia*, ed. Albert Seay (American Institute of Musicology, 1970), 2:1–3. Reprinted by permission of A. Carapetyan, Director, and Hänssler-Verlag. All rights reserved. International copyright secured.

Ahime, dov'è 'l bel viso,
In cui solea tener nid' amore,
E dove ripost'era ogni mia speme,
Ch'ornav'il mondo di splendore,
Il mio caro thesoro, il sommo bene?
Oime, chi me 'l ritien', chi me lo cela?

O fortuna, o mort'ingorda,
Cieca spietat'e sorda,
Chi m'ha tolto 'l mio cor, chi me l'asconde?

Dov'è 'l ben mio che più non mi risponde?

Alas, where is the pretty face
in which love used to nest
and where rested my every hope,
adorning the world with splendor,
my dear treasure, the highest good?
Alas, who keeps it from me, who hides it from
    me?

O luck, o greedy death,
blind, merciless and dumb.
Who has snatched away my heart, who hides it
    from me?

Where is my darling who answers me no
    more?

This madrigal of around 1538 illustrates two aspects of the genre, then in an
early stage of development. On the one hand, the homophonic motion, the
square rhythms, and the strict adherence to the form of the verse ally it to
the chanson and frottola. On the other hand, it is full of subtle expressive
touches. The descending minor thirds at the opening of the soprano melody,
harmonized by a descending cycle of fifths, portray the melancholy and hollow feeling of loss that the lover endures. The emotion-laden words "mio
caro thesoro" (my dear treasure, measures 21–24), are heightened by turning
from a C-major to a sustained B♭-major chord, which is outside the mode of
the piece and causes a cross-relation with the previous harmony. This clash
of harmonies, foreshadowed and enhanced by the alto's major sixth to the

bass going to the fifth in measures 4–5, serves as a kind of motto, recurring at measures 30–33, 45–46, and 50–51. The opening music returns slightly varied and set to different words at the end, beautifully preserving a unity of mood.

Arcadelt set the phrase "Oime, chi me'l ritiene" (Alas, who keeps it from me, measures 26–28) to a plaintive series of parallel sixth chords, the voices entering in imitation. The Roman Catholic reformer Bernardino Cirillo, who criticized the church music of this period for failing to move listeners with the message of the sacred texts, saw in this madrigal a ray of hope, a sign that composers would soon turn away from learned fugues to music's primary goal of communicating feeling.[1]

---

1. See his letter of 1549 in Lewis Lockwood, ed., *Palestrina, Pope Marcellus Mass,* Norton Critical Score (New York: Norton, 1975), p. 15.

38 ADRIAN WILLAERT (CA. 1490–1562)

Madrigal: *Aspro core e selvaggio*

Willaert, *Musica nova* (Venice, 1559). Willaert, *Opera omnia,* ed. Hermann Zenck and Walter Gerstenberg, vol. 13 (American Institute of Musicology, 1966), pp. 54–60.

Aspro core e selvaggio, e cruda voglia
In dolce, umile, angelica figura,
Se l'impreso rigor gran tempo dura,
Avran di me poco honorata spoglia:
Che, quando nasce e mor fior, erba e foglia,
Quando è 'l dí chiaro e quando è notte oscura,
Piango ad ogni hor. Ben ho di mia ventura,
Di madonna e d'Amore onde mi doglia.
Vivo sol di speranza, rimenbrando,
Che poco humor già per continua prova
Consumar vidi marmi e pietre salde.

Non è sí duro cor, che lagrimando,
Pregando, amando, talhor non si smova,
Né sì freddo voler, che non si scalde.
                        —FRANCESCO PETRARCA

Harsh heart and savage, and a cruel will
in a sweet, humble, angelic face,
if this adopted severity persist for long,
they will get from me spoils of little honor;
for when flower, grass, and leaf are born and die,
when it is shining day and when it is dark night,
I weep at every hour. Well may I grieve,
for my luck, my lady and my love.
I live by hope alone, remembering
that by continuous drops
I have seen little liquid consume marble and
    solid stones.
There is no heart so hard that weeping,
begging, loving sooner or later does not move,
nor so cold a resolve that it cannot be warmed.

This setting of a sonnet by Petrarch that Willaert probably composed in the mid-1540s was one of the pioneering works that helped to set the trend toward faithful text declamation and vivid expression. The composer probably knew the analysis Pietro Bembo had published in 1525 that demonstrated how Petrarch carefully suited the sound of the words to two worlds of feeling, the *grave* (serious, majestic) and the *piacevole* (charming, sweet). In the beginning of the sonnet, Petrarch expressed Madonna Laura's "harsh and savage heart" in a *grave* line, filled with double consonants and clipped, harsh sounds; he then described her "sweet, humble, angelic face" in a contrasting *piacevole* line made up of liquid, resonant, and sweet sounds.

Willaert's setting seems almost to grow out of Bembo's theory. For the first line (measures 1–10), Willaert lingered on the rawer consonances, emphasizing major sixths and thirds, including parallel major thirds, and favoring melodic motion in whole steps and major thirds. For the second line, he chose the sweeter consonances of minor thirds and minor sixths (realized through accidental flats), melodic motion by semitones and minor thirds, and simulated triple time to match Petrarch's deliberate arrangement of accented syllables. It is interesting that his pupil Zarlino counseled precisely these devices for attaining these emotional effects (see vignette in HWM, p. 198),[2] with the exception of parallel major thirds, of which he disapproved. For the first line Willaert gained a crude effect by repeatedly sliding from the major sixth to the fifth instead of resolving it to the octave, as was normally expected at this time.

Purely musical imagery provides contrasts in the line "Quando è 'l di chiaro" (when it is shining day) and "e quando è notte oscura" (and when it is dark night): in the first phrase, the parts ascend toward a clear C-major chord, while for the second the soprano drops an octave and descends through a B^b to a dark A-minor chord. Another musical shift differentiates between the hard heart (harsher major intervals) and the softening effect of tears (softer minor intervals) in measures 103 to 114. Willaert rendered the repeated weeping described in the half-line—"piango ad ogni hor" (I weep at every hour, measures 50–58)—by imitating or reworking sixteen times the motive introduced by the soprano.

The composer divided the fourteen lines of the sonnet into two sections, similar to the two *partes* of longer motets, the first setting the *ottava* or first eight lines, the second the *sestina* or final six lines. The first section ends on the fifth degree of the mode, the second on the final. Willaert was careful to devise his scheme of cadences according to the grammatical units of the poem. The first full cadence occurs at measure 36, coinciding with the text's colon (then equivalent to our modern semicolon). He avoided a cadence where the punctuation did not call for a stop.

---

2. Zarlino, *The Art of Counterpoint,* Ch. 57, p. 77–178; *Le institutioni harmoniche,* Book IV, Ch. 32, Strunk, *Source Readings,* 255-59 (= *The Renaissance,* 65–69), where this and four other madrigals from *Musica nova* are cited as models for the expression of various moods.

39 CIPRIANO DE RORE (1516–1565)

Madrigal: *Datemi pace, o duri miei pensieri*

Di Cipriano de Rore il secondo libro de madregali a quattro voci (Venice, 1557). Rore, *Opera omnia*, ed. Bernhard Meier, vol. 4 (American Institute of Musicology, 1969), pp. 73–75.

Datemi pace, o duri miei pensieri:	Give me peace, O my jarring thoughts.
Non basta ben ch'Amor Fortuna e Morte	Is it not enough that Love, Fate, and Death
Mi fanno guerra intorno, e 'n su le porte,	wage war all about me and at my very gates,
Senza trovarmi dentro altri guerrieri?	without finding other enemies within?
E tu, mio cor, ancor se' pur qual eri?	And you, my heart, are you still as you were?
Disleal a me sol; che fiere scorte	Disloyal to me alone: for you harbor fierce spies
Vai ricettando e se' fatto consorte	and have allied yourself
De' miei nemici si pronti e leggieri.	with my enemies, bold and brisk as they are.
In te i secreti suoi messaggi, Amore,	In you Love reveals his secret messages,
In te spiega Fortuna ogni sua pompa,	in you Fate boasts all her triumphs,
E Morte la memoria di quel colpo	and Death [awakens] the memory of that blow
Che l'avanzo di me convien che rompa;	which must surely destroy all that remains of me;
In te i vaghi pensier s'arman d'errore:	In you gentle thoughts arm themselves with falsity:
Perche d'ogni mio mal te solo incolpo.	Wherefore I charge you alone guilty of all my ills.

—FRANCESCO PETRARCA

In this madrigal, from Rore's second book of madrigals for four voices of 1557, the composer imbued every detail of the music with the sense and feeling of Petrarch's sonnet. The texture shifts between homophony and imitation, the temporal organization between triple and duple, and the note values between long and short, all depending on the immediate text.

The opposition in the first line between the sought-for peace and the painful thoughts that break into it is reflected in the contrast between the serene root-position harmonies and cheerful triple rhythms (as in popular songs or villanelle) of the first half of the line, "Datemi pace" (Give me peace), and the staggered rhythms, the bleak $^6_3$ and $^6_4$ chords, and the archaic fauxbourdon-like cadence of the second half of the line, "o duri miei pensieri" (O my jarring thoughts). The peaceful mood of the slow triple time of the opening is shattered by the galloping triple meter and the several sharps in measures 10 to 23 that represent the battle in the poet's mind. The galloping triplets reappear in measures 36 to 46, conspiring against the prevailing duple meter like "fierce spies."

Rore radically changed the texture between the first and second quatrains (measure 24). As the poet turned from addressing his thoughts to pleading with his heart, the music turns from homophony to loosely imitative texture, one voice after another crying out, "And you, my heart."

In striving to depict vividly the emotions of the text, Rore and his followers dared brash harmonic progressions, such as juxtaposition of chords whose roots are a third apart (measures 26–27), the normally prohibited chromatic step from B to B♭ (measures 55–56), or the sudden transitory modulations that touch distant points of the tonal spectrum (measures 58–62), where within a few measures the harmony wanders far from the keytone G into B major and F major.

Monteverdi must have had compositions such as this in mind when he credited Rore with starting a "seconda pratica," a new harmonic practice free of the restrictions of strict modal counterpoint.

Carlo Gesualdo (ca. 1561–1613)

Madrigal: *"Io parto" e non più dissi*

Gesualdo, *Madrigali a cinque voci libro sesto* (Gesualdo, 1611). *Sämtliche Madrigale für fünf Stimmen*, ed. Wilhelm Weismann, 1:29–32. © 1957 by Ugrino Verlag, Hamburg.: Assigned to VEB Deutscher Verlag für Musik, Leipzig.

a sì pie - to - si ac - cen - - - - - - ti.

a sì pie - to - si ac - cen - - - - - - ti.

a sì pie - to - si ac - cen - - - - ti.

a sì pie - to - si ac - cen - - ti, ac - - cen - - ti.

a sì pie - to - si ac - cen - - - - ti.

"Io parto" e non più dissi che il dolore Privò di vita il core. Allor proruppe in pianto e dissi Clori Con interrotti omèi: "Dunque ai dolori io resto. Ah, non fia mai Ch'io non languisca in dolorosi lai." Morto fui, vivo son che i spirti spenti tornaro in vita a sì pietosi accenti.	"I depart." I said no more, for grief robbed my heart of life. Then Clori broke out in tears and said, with interrupted cries of "Alas": "Hence I remain in pain. Ah, may I never cease to pine away in painful lays." Dead I was, now I am alive, for my spent spirits returned to life at the sound of such pitiable accents.

Chromaticism was for Gesualdo no mere affectation of antiquity but a deeply moving response to the text. For the lover's exclamation "Dunque ai dolori resto" (Hence I remain in pain, measures 20–23), Gesualdo combined melodic half-step motion with the ambiguous succession of chords whose roots are a third apart. He fragmented the poetic line, yet achieved continuity. He did this by avoiding conventional cadences and by running a thread through the labyrinth of chromaticism, emphasizing the main steps of the *E*-mode at beginnings and ends of lines and at pauses in the feverish activity—for example, measures 7 (*E*), 11 (*G*), 15 (*E*), 23 (*E*), 25 (*B*), 29 (*E*), and, of course, at the end (*E*).

The listener's attention nevertheless is drawn from this consistent structure to details. For instance, three distinct musical ideas make up the first line: the recitational "Io parto," a chromatic rise to a half-cadence for the speaker's admission that he said no more, and, third, an expression of pain through a descending line and a suspension, immediately intensified by a repetition a semitone higher that alters the descending whole steps to half steps (measure 6). Similarly, the second line is split into two: the simple recitation "Privò," and the descending imitative entries representing a heart breaking. When Clori speaks (measure 20), the three upper parts declaim against the bass, as the three lower parts had done for the opening male exclamation. The music of the penultimate line (measures 28 to 37) contains three separate images: of death, through a chromatic succession of sustained chords; of renewed life, through rapid motion, close imitation, and syncopation; and of exhaustion ("spirti spenti"—spent spirits), through an erratic subject whose descending imitations portray lassitude while the upward imitations suggest a gasping for air. In the final line Gesualdo indulges in a pun, setting the word "accenti" with ornamental runs of the kind that when improvised were called *accenti*.

Although first published in 1611, this madrigal may have been composed in the late 1590s.

CLAUDIO MONTEVERDI (1567–1643)

Madrigal: *Cruda Amarilli*

Monteverdi, *Il quinto libro de madrigali a cinque voci* (Venice, 1606). *Tutte le opere di Claudio Monteverdi,* ed. G. Francesco Malipiero (© Copyright 1929 by Universal Edition A.G., Vienna), 5:1–4. Copyright renewed. All rights reserved. Used by permission of European American Music Distributors Corp. Sole U.S. and Canadian Agent for Universal Edition, Vienna.

1) Nell'originale:

Cruda Amarilli che col nome ancora
D'amar, ahi lasso, amaramente insegni.
Amarilli del candido ligustro,
Più candida e più bella,
Ma dell'aspido sordo
E più sorda e più fera e più fugace.
Poi che col dir t'offendo
I mi morò tacendo.
       —GIOVANNI BATTISTA GUARINI

Cruel Amaryllis, who with your name
to love, alas, bitterly you teach.
Amaryllis, more than the white privet
pure, and more beautiful,
but deafer than the asp,
and fiercer and more elusive.
Since telling I offend you,
I shall die in silence.

The text of this madrigal, a speech from Giovanni Battista Guarini's *Il pastor fido*, is one of eleven in Monteverdi's fifth book of madrigals (1605) that are drawn from this pastoral verse play. Here, in the second scene from the first act, Mirtillo complains that Amaryllis is spurning his love. The speech begins with a pun on the name Amarilli, whose stem "amar" can be a contraction either of "amare" (to love) or "amaro" (bitter). With her name, Mirtillo protests, Amaryllis teaches how to love bitterly. Monteverdi seized the bitter mood of the opening words "Cruda Amarilli" with the canto's suspended seventh against the bass; this resolves in an even more biting dissonance, a minor ninth. The same pattern is then repeated a fourth higher. But then, echoing the text's sardonic humor, Monteverdi lightens the mood by setting the next half-line in a dancelike dotted rhythm that takes us without a pause into the next line, which mixes the jeering laughter of sixteenth notes with the crudest dissonances of the piece.

This madrigal was already in circulation in 1598, the date of an imaginary dialogue in which these violations of the contrapuntal rules for the treatment of dissonance were criticized in Giovanni Maria Artusi's *L'Artusi overo delle imperfettioni della moderna musica* (The Artusi, or Imperfections of Modern Music) of 1600. One interlocutor in the dialogue particularly

objected to measures 12–14, which he quoted,[3] pointing out that the soprano part in measure 13 failed to agree with the bass. The *A*, a ninth, appears
out of nowhere and leaps to a seventh, *F*. The other interlocutor in the dialogue defends the passage, arguing that if one imagines a *G* on the first beat
of the soprano part, the figure is like an *accento*, an improvised embellishment common at this time, replacing the stepwise motion *G–F–E* with
G–A–F–E. Such written-out embellishments, or diminutions, as they were
called, also season the harmony with runs in measure 12. The grating dissonances of measure 2 can also be explained as the diminution of the leaps
D–B and *B–G* in the upper parts. Although some of Monteverdi's dissonances may thus be rationalized as embellishments, their real motivation was
to convey through harmony, rather than through the graphic images of
some earlier madrigals, the meaning and feeling of the poet's message. In his
preface to the fifth book of madrigals of 1605, in which this composition
was published, Monteverdi called his approach a second practice (*seconda
pratica*) that set composers free to violate, for the sake of expressing a text,
some of the strict rules of the first practice taught in the manuals on counterpoint.

   Cruda Amarilli typifies the flexible, animated, evocative, and variegated
style of Monteverdi's polyphonic madrigals. It is rich in musical invention,
humorous yet sensitive, and audacious yet perfectly logical in its harmonies.

---

3. Strunk, *Source Readings*, p. 395 (= *The Baroque Era,* p. 33).

CLAUDIN DE SERMISY (CA. 1490–1562)

Chanson: *Tant que vivray*

Has sectional form is strophic

Tant que vivray en aage florissant.
Par plusieurs fois m'a tenu languissant.

Je serviray d'amours le roy puissant En fais en
Mais apres deul m'a faict rejoyssant Car j'ay l'a-

ditz en chansons et accordz. Son alliance
mour de la belle au gent corps.

Claudin de Sermisy, *Collected Works*, vol. 1, Chansons, ed. Gaston Allaire and Isabelle Cazeaux (American Institute of Musicology, 1974), pp. 99–100.

Tant que vivray en aage florissant,
Je serviray d'amours le roy puissant
En fais en ditz en chansons et accordz.
Par plusieurs fois m'a tenu languissant,
Mais apres deul m'a faict rejoyssant
Car j'ay l'amour de la belle au gent corps.

Son alliance
C'est ma fiance,
Son cueur est mien,
Le mien est sien.
Fy de tristesse,
Vive lyesse,
Puisqu'en amour a tant de bien.

As long as I am able-bodied,
I shall serve the potent king of love
through deeds, words, songs, and harmonies.
Many times he made me languish,
but after mourning, he let me rejoice,
because I have the love of the fair lady with
    the lovely body.

Her alliance
is my betrothal.
Her heart is mine,
mine is hers.
Shun sorrow.
Live in merriment,
because there is so much good in love.

Quand je la veulx servir et honorer,	When I want to serve and honor her,
Quand par escriptz veulx son nom decorer,	when I want to adorn her name with words,
Quand je la veoy et visite souvent,	when I see and visit her often,
Ses envieux n'en font que murmurer;	those jealous of her do nothing but whisper;
Mais nostre amour n'en scauroit moins durer;	but our love would not last any less,
Autant ou plus en emporte le vent,	however far the wind carries the rumors.
Maulgré envie,	Despite jealousy,
Toute ma vie,	all my life,
Je l'aymeray	I will love her
Et chanteray;	and sing of her;
C'est la premiere,	She is the first,
C'est la derniere	she is the last
Que j'ay servie	that I have served
Et serviray.	and will serve.

—CLÉMENT MAROT

This song belongs to the type usually known as the "Parisian chanson." Its lively, syllabic, mostly homophonic setting is true to this type. As in the frottola, the melody is in the top voice, and the harmony consists of thirds and fifths with only an occasional sixth. At the cadences, in place of a suspension, the note that becomes a dissonance (for example, the c'' in measure 3), is repercussed on the strong beat, giving an "appoggiatura" effect. The end of each line of text is marked off with a relatively long note or by repeated notes, so that the form of the poetry is clearly conveyed.

Again as in the frottola, the composer did not set out to illustrate the text in detail but to capture the good cheer and optimism of the poem. In any case, the strophic form does not lend itself to more specific expression.

43 CLAUDE LE JEUNE (1528/30–1600)

Chanson: *Revecy venir du printans*

RECHANT à 5

Le Printemps (Paris: Ballard, 1603), ed. Henry Expert in *Les maîtres musiciens de la Renaissance française*, 12 (Paris: Alphonse Leduc, 1900), pp. 11–27.

[1] CHANT à 2

Le cou _ rant des eaus re _ cher _ chant

Le cou _ rant des eaus re _ cher _ chant

Le ca _ nal d'é té s'é _ clair _ cît:

Le ca _ nal d'é té s'é _ clair _ cît:

Et la mer cal _ me de ces flots

Et la mer cal _ me de ces flots

A _ mo _ lit le tris _ te cour _ rous:

A _ mo _ lit le tris _ te cour _ rous:

Le Ca _ nard s'e _ gay _ e plon _ jant,

Le Ca _ nard s'e _ gay _ e plon _ jant,

RECHANT à 5

[2] CHANT à 3

RECHANT à 5

[3] CHANT à 4

A _ ni _ maus, qui vo _ let en l'air,

A _ ni _ maus, qui ram _ pet au chams,

A _ ni _ maus, qui na _ get auz eaus.

Ce qui mes _ me _ ment ne sent pas,

Ce qui mes _ me _ ment ne sent pas,

Ce qui mes _ me _ ment ne sent pas,

Ce qui mes _ me _ ment ne sent pas,

A _ mou _ reux se fond de plai _ zir.

A _ mou _ reux se fond de plai _ zir.

A _ mou _ reux se fond de plai _ zir.

A _ mou _ reux se fond de plai _ zir.

CE RESTE est à 5

(*) Dans l'original, par erreur:

Les é _ bas et

Tou _ te cho _ se rit de plai _ zir:
Tou _ te cho _ se rit de plai _ zir:
Tou _ te cho _ se rit de plai _ zir:
Tou _ te cho _ se rit de plai _ zir:
Tou _ te cho _ se rit de plai _ zir:

Sé _ le _ bron la gay _ e sai _ zon,
Sé _ le _ bron la gay _ e sai _ zon,
Sé _ le _ bron la gay _ e sai _ zon,
Sé _ le _ bron la gay _ e sai _ on,
                                    (*)
Sé _ le _ bron la gay _ e sai _ zon,

(*) Dans l'orig.

Revecy venir du Printans
L'amoureuz' et belle saizon.

Le courant des eaus recherchant
Le canal d'été s'éclaircît:
Et la mer calme de ces flots
Amolit le triste courrous:
Le Canard s'egaye plonjant,
Et se lave coint dedans l'eau;
Et la grû' qui fourche son vol
Retraverse l'air et s'en va.

Here again comes the Spring,
the amorous and fair season.

The currents of water that seek
the canal in summer become clearer;
and the calm sea the waves'
sad anger soothes.
The duck, elated, dives
and washes itself quietly in the water.
And the crane that branches off in flight
recrosses the air and flies away.

Revecy venir du Printans
L'amoureuz' et belle saizon.

Le Soleil éclaire luizant
D'une plus séreine clairté:
Du nuage l'ombre s'enfuit,
Qui se ioû' et court et noircît.
Et foretz et champs et coutaus
Le labeur humain reverdît,
Et la prê' découvre ses fleurs.

Revecy venir du Printans
L'amoureuz' et belle saizon.

De Venus le filz Cupidon
L'univers semant de ses trais,
De sa flamme va réchaufér,
Animaus, qui volet en l'air,
Animaus, qui rampet au chams,
Animaus, qui naget auz eaus.
Ce qui mesmement ne sent pas,
Amoureux se fond de plaizir.

Revecy venir du Printans
L'amoureuz' et belle saizon.

Rion aussi nous: et cherchon
Les ébas et ieus du Printans:
Toute chose rit de plaizir:
Sélebron la gaye saizon,

Revency venir du Printans
L'amoureuz' et belle saizon.

Revency venir . . .

Here again comes the Spring,
the amorous and fair season.

The sun shines brightly
with a calmer light.
The shadow of the cloud vanishes
from him who sports and runs and darkens.
Forests and fields and slopes
human labor makes green again,
and the prairie unveils its flowers.

Here again comes the Spring,
the amorous and fair season.

Cupid, the son of Venus
seeding the universe with his arrows,
with his flame he will rekindle
animals that fly in the air,
animals that crawl in the fields,
animals that swim in the seas.
Even those that feel not
in love they melt in pleasure.

Here again comes the Spring,
the amorous and fair season.

Let us, too, laugh, and let us seek
the sports and games of Spring:
everything smiles with pleasure;
let us celebrate the merry season.

Here again comes the Spring,
the amorous and fair season.

Here again comes . . .

The poets of the Académie de Poésie et de Musique (Academy of Poetry and Music), founded in 1570 under the patronage of King Charles IX, wrote strophic French verses in ancient classical meters (*vers mesurés à l'antique*), substituting for the modern stress accent the ancient Greek and Latin quantities of long and short syllables. Since the French language lacked any consistent distinction between long and short vowels, the theorists of *vers mesuré* worked out a system in which syllables were assigned long and short values, and composers set them accordingly.

In this poem the following pattern is used almost throughout: ◡◡– ◡– ◡––. In terms of quarter notes, this results in the pattern 2 3 3 2 2, which is identical to a popular hemiola rhythm used by Cara in his frottole and Monteverdi in his canzonets (see NAWM 36 and 56b). The refrain, or *rechant,* is for five voices, whereas the strophes, or *chants,* are for successively two, three, four, and five voices. Melismas, ordinarily of no more than four notes, relieve the uniformity of rhythm and add lightness and charm to the individual parts.

44 THOMAS WEELKES (CA. 1575–1623)

Madrigal: *O Care, thou wilt despatch me*

Ed. Nigel Davison in John Wilbye et al., *Neun englische Madrigale zu 5 und 6 Stimmen, Das Chorwerk* 132:37–44 (Wolfenbüttel: Möseler Verlag, 1983?).

2nd
Tercet

The presence of the syllables "fa-la" in this madrigal is deceptive, for the composer treats the first line of each tercet with extreme seriousness. Particularly notable is the opening, with its learned imitations in both direct and contrary motion and the chain of suspensions (including a diminished seventh at measure 3) to convey the poet's complaint. Weelkes evaded a resolution of this series of dissonances by turning away from the major triad on G in measure 7: the soprano moves to make a minor sixth with the bass, causing a diminished fourth with the tenor. He intensified the subsequent chain of suspensions by preparing two of the dissonances with a fourth. Weelkes's harmony is as intense and wry as Rore's or Gesualdo's, but the overall effect is one of suave vocality and broadly sweeping momentum. He achieved a smooth progression to the gleeful fa-las of the third line by introducing their music as early as the second line, producing the pattern ABB CDD.

JOHN DOWLAND (1562–1626)

Air: *Flow, my tears*

[handwritten annotations: "5 strophies — decending motive", "tablature = way of notating fingering"]

Dowland, *Second Booke of Songes* (London, 1600). *The English Lute Songs,* Series 1, ed. Edmund H. Fellowes, revised by Thurston Dart, 5–6 (London: Stainer & Bell, 1969), pp. 4–6. Reprinted by permission.

imitations

Among Dowland's songs best known to Elizabethans, *Flow, my tears,* from his *Second Booke of Ayres* of 1600, spawned a whole series of variations and arrangements with titles such as *Pavana Lachrymae* by William Byrd (NAWM 47). Most of Dowland's airs are strophic; this one is a compromise between strophic and through-composed. The first two stanzas are sung to the first strain; the next two to the second strain; and the final stanza has its own music; therefore musically the form is AABBCC. Thus it duplicates the pattern of the pavane, and it may have been conceived as a dance-song.

Clearly, concrete painting or expression of individual words and phrases is not possible under the circumstances, but Dowland captures the dark mood that pervades all five stanzas, particularly through the downward diatonic motion from *C* to *G#* which dominates each of the strains. One can speak in this music of modern tonalities. The first strain is in A minor, the second modulates from the relative major, C, to the dominant of A minor, and the third strain returns to A minor.

46 PIERRE ATTAINGNANT (CA. 1494–CA. 1552)
Danseries a 4 Parties, Second Livre

a) Basse danse (No. 1)

Note values reduced by half. Barlines through the entire brace mark the *quaternions* of the choreography; triple-time measures are set off by barlines through the staff; after every seventh minim of a *quaternion* a broken line appears. *Danseries a 4 parties, Second livre* (Paris, 1547), ed. Raymond Meylan (Paris: Heugel & Cie., ©1969), pp. 1, 38–39.

b) Branle gay: *Que je chatoulle ta fossette* (No. 36)

Attaingnant was not a composer but an editor and printer who issued many
collections of chansons and of dance music. The *basse danse* reached the
height of popularity in the fifteenth century. By the time Attaingnant's collection was published in 1547, it had almost disappeared. In the basse danse

of NAWM 46a, the pattern of beats, 3 4 2 3, is repeated throughout, while there is little melodic repetition.

One of the basic steps of the basse danse was the *branle*, a side step with a swaying shift of weight from the right to the left foot. The branle later became an independent dance and several varieties emerged. The *branle double* and *branle simple* were duple, while the *branle gay* was triple. The branle gay in NAWM 46b is consistently triple and is made up of a limited number of melodic four-measure phrases, some of which are inconclusive, others cadential, allowing for various antecedent-consequent combinations. The distribution of these phrases takes the overall shape of an A B A' form (A = measures 1–12; B = measures 13–28; A' = 29–48). Branles were often identified by the text that was sung to the top line, in this case *Que je chatoulle ta fossette*.

47 WILLIAM BYRD (1543–1623)

Pavana Lachrymae

The Fitzwilliam Virginal Book, ed. J. A. Fuller Maitland and W. Barclay Squire (Leipzig: Breitkopf & Härtel, 1899) 2:42–46.

Several composers wrote variations on John Dowland's air, *Flow, my tears*, among them Dowland himself. This song has the typical form of a pavane, which consists of three strains, each immediately repeated. Two measures of Byrd's keyboard arrangement are equal to one of Dowland's lute-and-voice original. Byrd added a variation after each strain. In the first statement of each strain Byrd retained the outline of the tune in the right hand while adding short accompanimental motives or decorative turns, figurations, and scale work imitated between the hands. In each of the variations, marked "Rep." in the score, the relationship to Dowland's model is more subtle. There are rhythmic displacements and the melody is less obvious, but the harmony is retained and the melody can usually be traced in some part of the texture. At the words "And tears and sighs and groans" (NAWM 45, mm. 11–12), where Dowland imitated the melody in his lute accompaniment, Byrd followed his example (mm. 32–33).

WILLIAM CORNYSH (CA. 1465–1523)

My love she mourneth

The tune first heard in the bass voice may be a preexistent one. Although the tenor then seems to sing a canon against the bass, in reality the tune is placed in the tenor, with contrapuntal lines composed above and below. This procedure resembles that of Continental song arrangements, but here the accompanying parts are markedly vocal and they contribute nice flourishes to the cadences.

Music at the Court of Henry VIII, transcribed and edited by John Stevens in *Musica Britannica* 18:23 (London: publ. for the Royal Musical Association by Stainer & Bell, Ltd 1962). © 1962, by The Musica Britannica Trust. Reproduced by permission of Stainer & Bell Ltd.

49 GIOVANNI DA PALESTRINA (CA. 1525–1594)

Pope Marcellus Mass

1567

a) Credo

Missarum Liber secundus (Rome, 1567): *Opere complete di Giovanni Pierluigi da Palestrina*, ed. Raffaele Casimiri (Rome: Edizione Fratelli-Scalera), 4 (1939): 177–87, 194–96. Reprinted by permission of the Istituto Italiano per la Storia Della Musica.

Credo

Credo in unum Deum, Patrem omnipotentem, factorem caeli et terrae, visibilium omnium et invisibilium. Et in unum Dominum Jesum Christum Filium Dei unigenitum. Et ex Patre natum ante omnia saecula. Deum de Deo, lumen de lumine, Deum verum de Deo vero. Genitum, non factum, consubstantialem Patri: per quem omnia facta sunt. Qui propter nos homines et propter nostram salutem descendit de caelis. Et incarnatus est de Spiritu Sancto ex Maria Virgine: et homo factus est. Crucifixus etiam pro nobis: sub Pontio Pilato passus, et sepultus est. Et resurrexit tertia die, secundum Scripturas. Et ascendit in caelum: sedet ad dexteram Patris. Et iterum venturus est cum gloria judicare vivos et mortuous: cujus regni non erit finis. Et in Spiritum Sanctum, Dominum, et vivificantem: qui ex Patre, Filioque procedit. Qui cum Patre, et Filio simul adoratur, et conglorificatur: qui locutus est per Prophetas. Et unam sanctam catholicam et apostolicam Ecclesiam. Confiteor unum baptisma in remissionem peccatorum. Et exspecto resurrectionem mortuorum. Et vitam venturi saeculi. Amen.

I believe in one God, Father Almighty, maker of heaven and earth and of all things visible and invisible. And in one Lord Jesus Christ, the only-begotten Son of God, born of the Father before all ages. God of God, light of light, true God of true God. Begotten, not made, being of one substance with the Father, by whom all things were made. Who for us men and for our salvation came down from heaven. And was made incarnate by the Holy Ghost of the Virgin Mary, and was made man. And was crucified for us under Pontius Pilate. He suffered and was buried. And the third day he rose again according to the Scriptures. And ascended into heaven, and sitteth on the right hand of the Father. And he shall come again with glory to judge the quick and the dead; of whose kingdom there shall be no end. And in the Holy Ghost, Lord and giver of life, who proceedeth from the Father and the Son. Who, together with Father and the Son, is worshiped and glorified; who spoke by the prophets. And one holy, Catholic, and Apostolic Church. I acknowledge one baptism for the remission of sins. And I look for the resurrection of the dead, and the life of the world to come. Amen.

b) Agnus Dei I

For a translation of the Agnus Dei, see NAWM 3.

The relation of this Mass to Pope Marcellus II, who reigned for twenty days in 1555, is uncertain. It is also not clear how the Mass relates to the reforms of the Council of Trent (1545–63), in which the use of polyphony in the church was discussed and deplored by some religious leaders. However, by adopting a transparent style of writing in this Mass, Palestrina countered the criticism that the text in much sacred polyphony could not be heard or understood.

The Credo is always a challenge to a composer because of the importance and length of the text. In this setting, Palestrina abandoned imitation for the sake of clear diction as well as brevity. The voices pronounce a given phrase, not in the staggered manner of imitative polyphony but simultaneously, etching the text in the hearer's consciousness. Palestrina could have employed *falsobordone*—a method that accomplishes this easily and that was used to harmonize the psalm tones in Italian and Spanish churches—as he did in his own *Improperia*. But he avoided its monotony by breaking up the six-voice choir into smaller groups, each with its particular tone color. He reserved the full six voices for climactic or particularly significant words, such as "per quem omnia facta sunt" (by whom all things were made) or "Et incarnatus est" (And was made incarnate). Other texts are sung by three, four, or five voices. Thus some voices do not sing some portions of the text, because there is very little of the usual imitation or repetition.

The section that begins at measure 13 illustrates this flexible approach to musical textures. The group C-A-Tɪɪ-Bɪ is answered by the group C-Tɪ-Tɪɪ-Bɪɪ singing the same words, "Et in unum Dominum." Each group pronounces a segment of text in speech rhythm and has its own cadence, in both cases a weak one based on the major sixth-to-octave succession. The "Filium Dei unigenitum" (only-begotten Son of God) is sung by a trio, symbolizing the three-in-one essence of the Trinity, but the texture is now different—it is fauxbourdon resurrected. Fauxbourdon was frowned upon by Willaert's school as crude and uncouth, but Palestrina applied it to great effect here and elsewhere in the Credo. With its sixths and thirds, it provides relief from the almost constant fifth-third combinations, and it also evokes an aura of a distant, more devout age. Palestrina conserved forward motion by postponing closure. At measure 27 there is a perfect cadence, but it is weakened by the third in the top voice. A truly final cadence is reserved for the end of the next five-voice section, at the phrase "de Deo vero" (measure 38).

Palestrina also avoided monotony by rhythmic means. Accented syllables may occur on any of the beats, and only after a cadence is the normal alternation of down- and upbeat restored. For example, in the section "Et in unum Dominum" the listener hears the following alternation of triple, duple, and single beat units: 3 2 2 3 3 3 3 1 3 2 2.

The text of the Agnus Dei presents a different challenge. It has few words, which must be stretched out to produce a piece of sufficient weight to close the Mass. The composer has ample time for leisurely fugal expositions and development of motives. Palestrina seized the opportunity to indulge in his customary imitative style. Each of the six voices has a chance to sing the opening subject in a fugal exposition that lasts fifteen measures. "Qui tollis peccata mundi" is treated with closer imitations (later fittingly called *stretto,* which means "tight"). Voices sometimes enter only a quarter note apart (minims in the original notation). Each voice places accented syllables on different beats, spinning out its line at its own pace. In plainchant, the Agnus is sung three times; the last time, the phrase "dona nobis pacem" replaces "miserere nobis." In Palestrina's Mass, the first two statements are combined in Agnus Dei I; the third statement, Agnus Dei II (omitted in this anthology) is scored for seven voices.

50 TOMÁS LUIS DE VICTORIA (1548–1611)
O magnum mysterium

a) Motet

Motet from Victoria, *Motectae* (Venice, 1572), ed. Higini Anglès, in Victoria, *Opera omnia* (Barcelona: Instituto español de musicología, 1965–68), Monumentos de la música española, 26:7–9; Mass from Victoria, *Missae . . . liber secundus* (Rome, 1592), ed. Felipe Pedrell, Victoria, *Werke* (Leipzig: Breitkopf & Härtel, 1902–13) 2:6–9.

O magnum mysterium, et admirabile
sacramentum, ut animalia
viderent Dominum natum,
iacentem in praesepio.
O beata Virgo,
cuius viscera meruerunt portare
Dominum Iesum Christum. Alleluia.

O great mystery and awesome
sacrament, that the animals
should see the Lord, newly born,
lying in the manger.
O blessed Virigin,
whose womb was worthy of bearing
the Lord Jesus Christ. Alleluia.

b) Mass: Kyrie

For the text of the Kyrie, see NAWM 3.

Like most of Victoria's Masses, this is based on one of his motets, *O magnum mysterium,* which was written for the feast of the Circumcision on January 1. The motet exploits a variety of textures and motives to express successively the mystery, wonder, and joy of the Christmas season.

The motet's fugal opening—paired entrances at the lower fifth, octave, and twelfth—is in strict Palestrina style, except for an expressive license in the subject, which, after an upward leap of a fifth, presses on in the same direction. The composer then turned to a declamatory delivery of the words "ut animalia viderent Dominum natum" (that the animals should see the Lord newly born), resuming the imitative method in the final clause of the sentence, "iacentem in praesepio" (lying in the manger). After a half-measure of silence, the entire choir solemnly exclaims, "O beata Virgo" (O blessed Virgin), the outer voices weaving a florid garland around the slower inner voices as they simultaneously pronounce "Virgo." A faster euphoric, triple-time, homophonic section articulates the exclamation "Alleluia," which continues to be reiterated in a melismatic coda that reverts to duple time.

In the Kyrie, Victoria reworked two of the motet's points of imitation. He converted the opening of the motet into a double fugue, using two related subjects fashioned from the motet's single subject. The Mass preserves the device of paired entrances and the harmonic relations between the voices. The Christe, as in other imitation Masses, utilizes a freely invented subject. On its return, the "Kyrie" borrows the music of the motet's "iacentem in praesepio" (measures 29–38), reworking the entrances and the counterpoint. Like Palestrina, Victoria strove for complete triadic harmony, although he preferred to end the Kyrie sections with the sound of the perfect consonances.

51 ORLANDO DI LASSO (1532–1594)

Motet: *Tristis est anima mea*

Sad is my soul

Masterpieces of Music Before 1750, ed. Carl Parrish and John F. Ohl (New York: Norton, 1951), pp. 80–85.

Tristis est anima mea usque ad mortem:
sustinete hic et vigilate mecum:
nunc videbitis turbam, quae
circumdabit me: vos fugam capietis,
et ego vadam immolari pro vobis.

Sad is my soul, even unto death;
abide here and watch with me;
soon you will see the crowd that
will encircle me; you will take flight,
and I shall go to be sacrificed for you.

This setting of the Respond for Maundy Thursday was published in 1565 and again in the *Magnus opus musicum*, a collection of Lasso's motets issued posthumously in 1604 by his sons. The text is based on the words of Jesus before he was crucified, as reported by Matthew (26:38) and Mark (14:34).

Lasso was famous in his own time for his forceful and imaginative projection of his texts. *Tristis est anima mea* is one of his most deeply moving and vivid settings. The descending-semitone motive, first heard in the bass on "Tristis" (sad) dominates the first nine measures. A consonant suspension in the first two measures prepares the more pungent dissonant suspension in the alto and the unusual suspension in the soprano, which resolves on the downbeat instead of the upbeat. This use of the suspension to achieve emotional tension rather than to prepare a cadence had become common in the mid-century madrigal but was still rare in sacred music. The word "mortem" (death) is underscored with a plagal cadence ending on a hollow chord lacking a third.

The next phrase of the text is split into two units because of their different connotations. "Sustinete" is interpreted not only in the sense of "abide" but also "hold up," for the harmony rises with hesitation in a series of fifths, sixths, and thirds among the parts. The fast motion at "vigilate" (watch out), on the other hand, suggests wakefulness (Jesus reproached his disciples several times for falling asleep on their watch). Lasso avoided a proper cadence at the end of this section (measure 27) to open the way for the declamatory proclamation "nunc videbis" (soon you will see), repeated with increasing fervor at a higher pitch and with fuller sound.

Lasso now resorted to madrigalistic word-painting for "circumdabit me" (will encircle me), illustrated by a circular melodic figure imitated in all the parts, and for "vos fugam capietis" (you will take flight), portrayed by a fugal stretto in which the subject takes off eleven times (like the eleven disciples who ran away when the twelfth, Judas, joined the angry crowd that beat and captured Jesus). Once again Lasso avoided a cadence, impatient to proclaim, note-against-note in all the voices, "et ego vadam immolari pro vobis" (and I shall go to be sacrificed for you).

To end the motet (measure 60), the composer returned to imitation, by both direct and contrary motion, stepping up the pace to the semiminim level (eighth notes in the transcription), over a pedal point, as if to suggest a sprinkling of grains of wheat (*mola*) over the sacrificial victim (the original meaning of *immolare*). Fittingly, this surge of activity leads to the only really full cadence in the work, marking the only period in the Latin text. Thus the words of the respond stimulated not only the rhythms, accents, and contours of the musical motives but the composer's every gesture: harmonic effects, textures, constructive devices such as suspensions and fugal imitation, the weight and placement of cadences, and, of course, clever allusions.

WILLIAM BYRD

Full Anthem: *Sing joyfully unto God*

The Byrd Edition, Vol. 11: *The English Anthems*, ed. Craig Monson (London: Stainer & Bell Ltd., 1983), pp. 82–90. Reproduced by permission. The pitch has been transposed up a major third from C to E♭ to conform with how, it is believed, the original scheme of clefs was read.

This setting of the first four verses of Psalm 81 was one of the most popular of Byrd's anthems. It belongs to the category of full anthem, which is the English equivalent of a choral motet, as opposed to the verse anthem, which was scored for soloists with instrumental accompaniment. Some of the sources for the full anthems include an organ accompaniment, but it is probably not by Byrd.

A comparison with the compositional methods of Palestrina, Lasso, and Victoria helps isolate the traits that are distinctively Byrd's. Cadences are more frequent, imitation is almost constant but freer, homophony is rare, and the voice lines are more angular and energetic.

The cadences, limited to the tonic and dominant (apart from one on the dominant of the dominant in measure 23), make the structure clear and anchor the work solidly in the major mode. The opening point of imitation, involving only four of the six parts, treats the subject freely, answering the rising fifth with a second, fourth, and octave. Vigorous leaps, such as Byrd and Lasso used more often than the other two composers, bring to life such texts as "Sing loud" (measures 10ff.) or "Take the song, and bring forth the timbrel" (tenor, measures 16ff.). A line made up almost entirely of leaps—even two successive rising fourths (the bass at measure 14)—is not unusual. A conspicuous evocation of the text stands out in the fanfares at "Blow the trumpet in the new moon" (measures 30–38). Homophonic texture is infrequent. The vertical harmony at measures 50–54 must have been inspired by the text "For this is a statute." Similarly, the music on the final line, "and a law of the God of Jacob," illustrates the idea of rule through a long fugal section.

Byrd paid close attention to the rhythm of the words as well as their meaning. Unstressed syllables are pronounced or begin on weak beats. Stressed syllables fall on the down- or upbeat of the *alla breve* measure (whole notes of the transcription) or are accented by syncopation.

Emilio de' Cavalieri (1550–1602)

Madrigal: *Dalle più alte sfere*

Intermedii et concerti, fatti per la commedia rappresentata in Firenze nelle nozze del Serenissimo Don Ferdinando Medici, e Madama Christiana di Loreno, Gran Duchi di Toscana (Venice, 1591). Ed. D. P. Walker, *Musique des intermèdes de "La Pellegrina"* (Paris: Éditions du Centre national de la recherche scientifique, 1963), pp. 2–8. The footnotes refer to the "Ninth" partbook (*Nono*), which has the instrumental parts and the text. The text is also given in the official description of the event: Bastiano de' Rossi, *Descrizione dell'apparato e degl'Intermedi fatti per la commedia rappresentata in Firenze nelle nozze de' Serenissimi Don Ferdinando Medici e Madama Cristina di Loreno* (Florence, 1589).

*On the recording, "autre terminaison" (p. 263) is inserted here.

Dalle più alte sfere	From the highest spheres
Di celesti sirene amica scorta	of the heavenly sirens, a friendly escort,
Son l'armonia ch'a voi vengo mortali,	I am Harmony, who comes to you mortals,
Poscia, che fino al ciel battendo l'ali	since even high in the sky, beating its wings,
L'alta fiama n'apporta,	lofty fame brought news
Che mai si nobil coppia 'l sol non vide	that never so noble a couple the sun did see
Qual voi nova Minerva e fort'Alcide.	as you, new Minerva and brave Hercules.
—GIOVANNI DE' BARDI	

The most costly and spectacular of the entertainments for the wedding of Grand Duke Ferdinand de' Medici of Tuscany and Christine of Lorraine in 1589 in Florence were the intermedi for Girolamo Barbagli's comedy, *La Pellegrina*. The intermedi—independent musical scenes before, between, and after the three-act comedy—had as their common theme the powers of ancient Greek music. They were produced by Emilio de' Cavalieri and directed by Giovanni Bardi (1534–1612). The solo madrigal *Dalle più alte sfere*, in honor of the wedding couple, opens the first intermedio, on the subject of the music of the spheres. Composed on a poem by Bardi, it is credited to Cavalieri in Bastiano de' Rossi's official chronicle. (The score, published in 1591, ascribes the music to Antonio Archilei, who may have been responsible only for the embellished voice part.) Quite typical of the solo songs of this period, it is scored for four parts, only the highest of which is intended to be sung. The singer, however, is given a very much ornamented version, while the simple version and the other three parts are assigned to instruments.

The style of writing is akin to that of the frottola: simple homophonic texture with a cadence at the end of each line. But the impression it makes is altogether different because of the virtuoso runs and cadenzas, which give us a sample of the brilliant improvisation that a well-trained singer could carry off. In the 1589 performance the work was sung by the most famous soprano of that time, Vittoria Archilei, who in this tableau represents the Dorian harmonia (or mode), as she makes her entrance on a cloud, surrounded by two other clouds holding the other six Greek harmoniae (see the illustration in HWM, p. 277). After she sings, the stage is filled with more clouds containing Necessity and the three Fates, who with a diamond spindle turn the celestial spheres—the planets and the stars—to which she refers in her song (see the illustration in HWM, p. 276).

Following her song are a sinfonia and three madrigals—the first and third for six voices, the second for three five-voice choruses—by Cristofano Malvezzi on poems by Ottavio Rinuccini.

GIULIO CACCINI (CA. 1550–1618)

Madrigal: *Perfidissimo volto*

Trilli – rapid repitition of same pitch

Perfidissimo volto,	O, most perfidious face,
Ben l'usata bellezza in te si vede	true, the usual beauty in you is seen,
Ma non l'usata fede.	but not the usual fidelity.
Già mi parevi dir: Quest'amorose	Once you seemed to say: "These amorous
Luci che dolcemente	eyes that sweetly
Rivolgo a te, sì bell'e sì pietose	I turn towards you, so beautiful and so
	compassionate—
Prima vedrai tu spente,	first you will see these lights extinguished
Che sia spento il desio ch'a te le gira.	before is spent the desire that they convey."
Ahi, che spento è 'l desio,	Alas, now spent is that desire,
Ma non è spento quel per cui sospira	but not spent is that for which sighs
L'abbandonato core!	the abandoned heart!
O volto troppo vago e troppo rio,	O face too lovely and too cruel,
Perchè se perdi amore	why when you lose love,
Non perdi ancor' vaghezza	do you not lose also loveliness,
O non hai pari alla beltà fermezza?	and why do you not match beauty with constancy?
—GIOVANNI BATTISTA GUARINI	

Caccini boasted in his foreword to *Le nuove musiche* that this madrigal was received "with affectionate applause" in Bardi's Camerata around 1590. Each line of poetry is set as a separate phrase, ending either in a cadence or a sustained note or pair of notes. This convention and the many repeated notes in speech rhythm were characteristic of the airs improvised on melodic formulas throughout the sixteenth century. At a number of the cadences Caccini wrote into the score embellishments of the kind that singers were accustomed to add—for example, at the words, "te le gira"(measures 29–31) and "non hai pari alla beltà fermezza?" (measures 56–60 and 71–77). Caccini wrote out the ornaments because he did not trust singers to invent appropriate ones of their own. Other refinements that Caccini considered essential to performance, described in his foreword to *Le nuove musiche* but not indicated in the score, are crescendos and decrescendos, trills and turns (called *gruppi* or *groppi*), rapid repetitions of the same pitch (called *trilli*), *esclamazioni*—decrescendo after attacking a note, then sforzando—and departures from strict observance of the printed note values, or what we call *tempo rubato*. The editor has suggested the placement of some of these effects in brackets.

Caccini borrowed dramatic gestures from the polyphonic madrigal: at "Ahi" (measure 32), where he broke off the line, then continued in speech-like rhythm; and at "O volto" (measure 46), where the melody drops a fifth, then a third, and reaches for a minor sixth. The text and music of the last lines are repeated, as was customary in the polyphonic madrigal.

55 JACOPO PERI (1561–1633)

Le musiche sopra l'Euridice

a) Prologue, Tragedy: *Io, che d'alti sospir*

PROLOGUE: TRAGEDY

1. Io, che d'alti sospir vaga e di pianti,
   Spars' or di doglia, hor di minaccie il volto,
   Fei negl'ampi teatri al popol folto
   Scolorir di pietà volti e sembianti.

   I, who with deep sighs and tears am smitten,
   my face, covered now with grief, now with menace,
   once in ample theatres crowded with people
   made their faces turn pale with pity.

2. Non sangue sparso d'innocenti vene,
   Non ciglia spente di tiranno insano,
   Spettacolo infelice al guardo umano,
   Canto su meste e lagrimose scene.

   Not of blood spilled from innocent veins,
   nor of eyes put out by an insane tyrant,
   but a spectacle unhappy to the human sight,
   do I sing on this sad and tearful stage.

3. Lungi via, lungi pur da' regi tetti
   Simulacri funesti, ombre d'affanni:
   Ecco i mesti coturni e i foschi panni
   Cangio, e desto ne i cor più dolci affetti.

   Stay far from under this royal roof,
   dismal images, shadows of anguish.
   Behold, the gloomy buskins and the dark rags
   I transform, and awaken in the hearts sweeter
   affections.

Note values reduced by half. Original barring retained. Time signatures added by the editor are in brackets; editorial accidentals are above the staff. In the Prologue, the composer intended that rhythmic adjustments be made in the strophes. Peri, *Le musiche sopra l'Euridice* (Florence, 1601), pp. 2, 11–12, 14–17.

4. Hor s'avverrà che le cangiate forme
   Non senza alto stupor la terra ammiri.

   Tal ch'ogni alma gentil ch'Apollo inspiri
   Del mio novo cammin calpesti l'orme,

5. Vostro, Regina, fia cotanto alloro,
   Qual forse anco non colse Atene, o Roma,
   Fregio non vil su l'onorata chioma,
   Fronda Febea fra due corone d'oro.

6. Tal per voi torno, e con sereno aspetto
   Ne' reali Imenei m'adorno anch'io,
   E su corde più liete il canto mio
   Tempro, al nobile cor dolce diletto.

7. Mentre Senna real prepara intanto
   Alto diadema, onde il bel crin si fregi

   E i manti e' seggi de gl'antichi regi,
   Del Tracio Orfeo date l'orecchie al canto.

Now, if it should happen that the changed forms
not without great amazement the world should
   admire,
so that every gentle genius that Apollo inspires
takes up the tracks of my new path,

Yours, Queen, will be so much laurel
that perhaps not even Athens or Rome won more,
no mean ornament on the honored head,
a leafy branch of Phoebus between two crowns.

Thus for you I return, and with a serene countenance
at this royal wedding I too adorn myself,
and with happier notes my song
I temper, for the noble heart's sweet delight.

Meanwhile the royal Seine prepares
a lofty diadem with which the beautiful hair to
   crown
and the cloaks and thrones of ancient kings;
to the song of the Thracian Orpheus, lend your ears.

b) Tirsi: *Nel pur ardor*

TIRSI

Nel pur ardor della più bella stella
Aurea facella di bel foc'accendi,
E qui discendi su l'aurate piume,
Giocondo Nume, e de celeste fiamma
L'anime infiamma.

Lieto Imeneo d'alta dolcezza un nembo
Trabocca in grembo a' fortunati amanti
E tra bei canti di soavi amori
Sveglia nei cori una dolce aura, un riso
Di Paradiso.

With the pure flame of the brightest star
light the golden torch with beautiful fire
and here descend on golden wings,
o happy God, and with celestial fire
the souls inflame.

Happy Hymen, let your shower of lofty sweetness
overflow into the breasts of the fortunate lovers
and, amidst pretty songs of delightful loves,
stir in their hearts a gentle breeze, a smile
of Paradise.

c) Dafne: *Per quel vago boschetto*
Arcetro: *Che narri, ohimè*
Orfeo: *Non piango e non sospiro*

più mi - se-ro a-man - te, Spet - ta - col di mi - se - ria e di tor - men - to! Non

pian - go e non sos - pi - ro, O mia ca - ra Eu - ri - di - ce, Ché sos - pi - rar,___

ché la - cri - mar non pos - so. Ca - da - ve - ro in - fe - li - ce, O___ mio co - re o mia

spe - me, o pa - ce o vi - ta! Ohi - mè, chi___ mi t'ha tol - to, Chi mi t'ha

tol - to o - hi - mè!___ do - ve sei gi - ta?

DAFNE

Per quel vago boschetto,	In the beautiful thicket,
Ove, rigando i fiori,	where, watering the flowers,
Lento trascorre il fonte degl'allori,	slowly courses the spring of the laurel,
Prendea dolce diletto	she took sweet delight
Con le compagne sue la bella sposa,	with her companions—the beautiful bride—
Chi violetta o rosa	as some picked violets, others roses,
Per far ghirland' al crine	to make garlands for their hair,
Togliea dal prato o dall'acute spine,	in the meadow or among the sharp thorns.
E qual posand' il fianco	Another, lying on her side
Su la fiorita sponda	on the flowered bank,
Dolce cantava al mormorar dell' onda;	sang sweetly to the murmur of the waves.
Ma la bella Euridice	But the lovely Eurydice
Movea danzando il piè sul verde prato	dancingly moved her feet on the green grass
Quand'ahi ria sorte acerba,	when—o bitter, angry fate!
Angue crudo e spietato	a snake, cruel and merciless,
Che celato giacea tra fiori e l'erba	that lay hidden among flowers and grass
Punsele il piè con si maligno dente,	bit her foot with such an evil tooth
Ch'impalidì repente	that she suddenly became pale
Come raggio di sol che nube adombri.	like a ray of sunshine that a cloud darkens.
El dal profondo core,	And from the depths of her heart,
Con un sospir mortale,	a mortal sigh,
Si spaventoso ohimè sospinse fuore,	so frightful, alas, flew forth,
Che, quasi avesse l'ale,	almost as if it had wings;
Giunse ogni Ninfa al doloroso suono.	every nymph rushed to the painful sound.
Et ella in abbandono	And she, fainting,
Tutta lasciossi all'or nell'altrui braccia.	let herself fall in another's arms.
Spargea il bel volto e le dorate chiome	Then spread over her beautiful face and her golden tresses
Un sudor viè più fredd'assai che giaccio.	a sweat colder by far than ice.

Indi s'udio 'l tuo nome	And then was heard your name, sounding
Tra le labbra sonar fredd'e' tremanti	between her lips, cold and trembling,
E volti gl'occhi al cielo,	and her eyes turned to heaven,
Scolorito il bel volto e' bei sembianti,	her beautiful face and mien discolored,
Restò tanta bellezza immobil gielo.	this great beauty was transformed to motionless ice.

ARCETRO

Che narri, ohimè, che sento?	What do you relate, alas, what do I hear?
Misera Ninfa, e più misero amante,	Wretched nymph, and more unhappy lover,
Spettacol di miseria e di tormento!	spectacle of sorrow and of torment!

ORFEO

Non piango e non sospiro,	I do not weep, nor do I sigh,
O mia cara Euridice,	o my dear Eurydice,
Ché sospirar, ché lacrimar non posso.	for I am unable to sigh, to weep.
Cadavero infelice,	Unhappy corpse,
O mio core, o mia speme, o pace, o vita!	o my heart, o my hope, o peace, o life!
Ohimè, chi mi t'ha tolto,	Alas, who has taken you from me?
Chi mi t'ha tolto, ohimè! dove sei gita?	Who has taken you away, alas? Where have you gone?
Tosto vedrai ch'in vano	Soon you will see that not in vain
Non chiamasti morendo il tuo consorte.	did you, dying, call your spouse.
Non son, non son lontano:	I am not far away;
Io vengo, o cara vita, o cara morte.	I come, o dear life, o dear death.

—OTTAVIO RINUCCINI

Euridice, on a text by Ottavio Rinuccini (1562–1621), with music by Jacopo Peri, is the earliest opera to survive in a complete score. It was produced for the wedding in 1600 of Henry IV of France and Maria de' Medici in Florence (though the music for some of the parts was then replaced by Caccini's version) and published the following year.

The three excerpts from Peri's *Euridice* illustrate three styles of monody found in this work. Only one of the styles is truly new. The Prologue (a) is modeled on the strophic aria for singing verses as practiced throughout the sixteenth century. Each line of verse is sung to a melodic scheme that consists of a repeated pitch and a cadential pattern ending in two sustained notes. A ritornello separates the strophes.

Tirsi's song (b) is also a kind of aria, but it is markedly rhythmic and tuneful, and the cadences at the ends of lines are harmonically stronger, being mostly dominant–tonic. It is framed by a "symphony" that despite its brevity is the longest purely instrumental interlude in the score.

Finally, Dafne's speech and the reactions to it of Arcetro and Orfeo (c) are true examples of the new recitative. The chords specified by the basso continuo and its figures have no rhythmic profile or formal plan and are there only to support the voice's recitation, which is free to imitate the rhythms of speech. The voice returns frequently to pitches consonant with the harmony on the main accents of the poetic line, but it wanders from the chordal tones of the accompaniment on syllables that would not be sustained in a spoken recitation. Only some line endings are marked by cadences; many are elided.

In the midst of preparations for the wedding of the legendary musician Orfeo and the nymph Euridice, Dafne reports that Euridice, while picking flowers to make a garland for her hair, was bitten by a snake and died. There is a natural progression in Dafne's speech; at first it is emotionally neutral, consonant, and slow-changing harmonically. As she tells of Euridice's fatal snakebite, it becomes more excited, with more dissonances, sudden changes of harmony, and fewer cadences, and the bass moves more quickly.

The responses to the news by Arcetro and Orfeo are also in the new recitative style but made more lyrical by the melodic construction with quasi-repetitions and sequences.

56 CLAUDIO MONTEVERDI
L'Orfeo

a) Prologue, La Musica: *Dal mio Permesso*

Dal mio permesso a_ma_to a voi ne

ve _ gno in_cli_ti e_roi san_gue gen_til de Re_gi di

cui nar_ra la fa_ma ec_cel_si pre_gi ne

giun _ ge al ver perch'è trop_p'al _ to il se _ _ gno.

Ritornello

Io la mu_si_ca son ch'ai dol_ci ac_cen_ _ _ti so far tranquil_lo

o_gni tur_ba_ _to co_ _re et hor di no_bi_l'i_ra et hor d'a_

_mo_re pos_ _ _ _s'in_fiammar le più ge_la_ _te men_ti.

Ritornello

Io su ce_te_ra d'or cantan_do so _ glio mor_tal o_rec_chio

lu_sin_gar ta_l'ho_ra e in que_sta gui _ sa a l'ar_mo_

_nia so_no_ra de la li _ ra del ciel più l'al _ me in_vo_glio.

Ritornello

Quin _ ci a dir _ vi d'Orfeo de _ sio mi spro _ _ na, d'Or _ feo che tras _ se

al suo can _ tar le fe _ re e ser _ vo fe' l'In _ fer _ no a sue pre _

_ ghie _ re Glo _ ria immortal di Pin _ do e d'E _ li _ co _ na.

Ritornello

Hor mentre i canti al ter _ no   hor lie _ ti hor me _ sti   non si mo _ va

Au _ gel _ lin   fra que _ ste pian _ te   ne s'o _ da

in que _ ste ri _ ve on _ da so _ nan _ te   _ et o _ gni au _ _ret _ ta   in suo cam _ min   s'ar _ re _   _ sti.

Ritornello

MUSIC

Dal mio Permesso amato a voi ne vegno,	From my beloved Permessus I come to you,
Incliti Eroi, sangue gentil de' Regi	Illustrious heroes, noble blood of kings,
Di cui narra la Fama eccelsi pregi,	of whom Fame relates their lofty worth,
Ne giunge al ver perch'è tropp'alto il segno.	yet falls short of the truth because the standard
	is too high.
Io la Musica son, ch'ai dolci accenti	I am Music, who, through sweet accents
So far tranquillo ogni turbato core,	know how to quiet every troubled heart,
Et hor di nobil' ira et hor d'amore	now with noble ire and now with love,
Poss' infiammar le più gelate menti.	I can inflame the most frozen spirtits.
Io su cetera d'òr cantando soglio	I, on a kithara of gold am used to singing,
Mortal orecchio lusingar tal'hora	charming mortal ears on occasion,
E in questa guisa a l'armonia sonora	and in this guise to the sonorous harmony
De la lira del ciel più l'alme invoglio.	of the heavenly lyre, the spirits beguile.
Quinci a dirvi d'Orfeo desio mi sprona,	Hence to tell you of Orpheus the desire spurs me:
D'Orfeo che trasse al suo cantar le fere	of Orpheus, who with his singing attracted the beasts,
E servo fè l'Inferno a sue preghiere	and made a servant of Hell with his pleas,
Gloria immortal di Pindo e d'Elicona.	immortal glory of Pindus and Helicon.
Hor mentre i canti alterno hor lieti, hor mesti,	Now while I alternate happy and sad songs,
Non si mova augellin fra queste piante,	not a bird moves among these trees,
Ne s'oda in queste rive onda sonante,	nor is heard on these shores a resounding wave,
Et ogni auretta in suo cammin s'arresti.	and every little breeze arrests its course.

b) Act II, Orfeo: *Vi ricorda* (excerpt)

ORPHEUS

Vi ricorda, o boschi ombrosi,
de' miei lungh' aspri tormenti,
quando i sassi ai miei lamenti
rispondean, fatti pietosi?

Do you recall, o shady woods,
my long, bitter torments,
when the stones to my laments
replied, pitiable deeds?

c) Messenger: *In un fiorito prato*
   Orfeo: *Tu se' morta*
   Chorus: *Ahi caso acerbo*

-ra fra l'erbe asco_so, le pun_se un piè con ve_le_no_so den_te.

Ed ec_co imman_ti_nente sco_lo_rir_si il bel vi_so

e nei suoi lumi sparir que lam_pi ond'ella al sol fea scor_no al_

_l'hor noi tut_te sbi_got_ti_te e me_ste le fummo intor_no ri_chia_

_mar tentando li spir_ti in lei smarri_ti con l'onda fresca e con possen_ti carmi, ma nul_la val_sè ahi las _ sa ch'el_la i langui_di lu _ mi alquan_to apren_

_do e te chiamando Orfe _ o, Or_fe _ o Do_po un gra _ ve so_

_spi _ ro spi _ rò fra queste braccia ed io ri_ma _ si piena il cor di pie_

_ta _ de e di spa_ven_to.

PASTORE

Ahi ca_so acer_bo ahi fat'empio e crude _ le, Ahi

stel_le ingiu_rio _ se, ahi ciel a_va _ ro.

PASTORE

A l'a_ma _

_ra novel_la rassembral'infeli _ce un mu_to sas_so che per trop_po do_lor non

può do_ler_si; Ahi ben havrebbe un cor di Tigre o d'Orsa chi non sentis_se

del tuo mal pie_ta_te, pri_vo d'ogni tuo ben mi_se_ro a_man_te.

ORFEO 54 19

Tu se' mor_ta se' mor_ta mia vi

Un organo di legno e un chitarone

_ta ed io respi__ro, tu se' da me par_ti_ta,

MESSENGER

In un fiorito prato	In a flowered meadow
Con l'altre sue compagne	with her companions
Giva cogliendo fiori	she was going about gathering flowers
Per farne una ghirlanda a le sue chiome,	to make a garland for her hair,
Quand'angue insidioso,	when a treacherous serpent
Ch'era fra l'erbe ascoso,	that was hidden in the grass
Le punse un piè con velenoso dente:	bit her foot with venomous tooth:
Ed ecco immantinente	Then at once
Scolorirsi il bel viso e nei suoi lumi	her face became pale, and in her eyes
Sparir que lampi, ond'ella al sol fea scorno.	those lamps that vied with the sun grew dim.
All'hor noi tutte sbigottite e meste	Then we all, frightened and sad,
Le fummo intorno, richiamar tentando	gathered around calling, tempting
Li spirti in lei smarriti	the spirits that were smothered in her
Con l'onda fresca e con possenti carmi;	with fresh water and powerful songs.
Ma nulla valse, ahi lassa!	But nothing helped, alas,
Ch'ella i languidi lumi alquanto aprendo,	for she, opening her languid eyes slightly,

E te chiamando Orfeo,
Dopo un grave sospiro
Spirò fra queste braccia, ed io rimasi
Piena il cor di pietade e di spavento.

called to you, Orpheus,
and, after a deep sigh,
expired in these arms, and I remained
with heart full of pity and terror.

SHEPHERD

Ahi caso acerbo, ahi fat' empio e crudele!
Ahi stelle ingiuriose, ahi cielo avaro!

Ah, bitter event, ah, wicked fate and cruel!
Ah, malicious stars, ah, greedy heavens!

A l'amara novella
rassembra l'infelice un muto sasso,
che per troppo dolor non può dolersi.
Ahi ben havrebbe un cor di Tigre o d'Orsa
Chi non sentisse del tuo mal pietate,
Privo d'ogni tuo ben, misero amante!

The bitter news
has turned the unfortunate one into a mute stone;
from too much pain, he can feel no pain.
Ah, he must have the heart of a tiger or a bear
who did not feel pity for your loss,
as you are bereft of your dear one, wretched lover.

ORPHEUS

Tu se' morta, mia vita, ed io respiro?
Tu se' da me partita
Per mai più non tornare, ed io rimango?
No, che se i versi alcuna cosa ponno,
N'andrò sicuro a' più profondi abissi,
E intenerito il cor del Re de l'Ombre
Meco trarrotti a riveder le stelle,
O se ciò negherammi empio destino
Rimarrò teco in compagnia di morte,
A dio terra, a dio cielo, e sole, a dio.

You are dead, my life, and I still breathe?
You have departed from me,
never to return, and I remain?
No, for if verses have any power
I shall go safely to the most profound abyss,
and having softened the heart of the King of the Shades
I shall bring you back to see the stars once again,
and if this is denied me by wicked fate,
I shall remain with you in the company of death.
Farewell earth, farewell sky and sun, farewell.

CHORUS

Ahi caso acerbo, ahi fat'empio e crudele!
Ahi stelle ingiuriose, ahi cielo avaro!
Non si fidi huom mortale
Di ben caduco e frale
Che tosto fugge, e spesso
A gran salita il precipizio è presso.

Ah, bitter event, ah, wicked fate and cruel!
Ah, malicious stars, ah greedy heavens!
Trust not, mortal man,
in goods fleeting and frail,
for they easily slip away, and often
after a steep ascent the precipice is near.

—ALESSANDRO STRIGGIO

Monteverdi's *Orfeo* was first performed in 1607 for the Accademia degli Invaghiti in Mantua. Alessandro Striggio (ca. 1573–1630), son of a Florentine musician and composer, expanded the story told by Rinuccini into a five-act play.

It is instructive to consider three sections from *Orfeo* that are more or less parallel to those selected from *Euridice*: the Prologue (a), Orfeo's song (b), the Messenger's narration of Euridice's death, and the reactions of the shepherds, Orfeo, and the chorus (c). It is immediately obvious that the whole is very much expanded. The ritornello for the Prologue is carefully scored, and although the Prologue itself is patterned on the air for singing poetry, Monteverdi wrote out each strophe, varying the melody while leaving the harmony intact, a technique practiced in the sixteenth century in the improvised singing of poetry.

Orfeo's strophic canzonet, *Vi ricorda o boschi ombrosi* (b), resembles in spirit Peri's aria for Tirsi, but the ritornello is worked out in five-part counterpoint. Again the idiom is a traditional one: the hemiola rhythm is the same as that in Cara's frottola *Io non compro più speranza* (NAWM 36), and the harmonization with root-position chords is also similar.

As in Peri's work, the most modern style is reserved for dramatic dialogue and impassioned speeches. In the Messagera's (messenger's) speech, *In un fiorito prato* (c), Monteverdi imitated the recitative style developed by Peri, but he shaped the melodic contour and the harmonic movement along broader lines. In Orfeo's lament, which follows, Monteverdi attained a new height of lyricism that leaves the first monodic experiments far behind. In the passage that begins "Tu se' morta," each phrase of music, like each phrase of text, builds upon what precedes and intensifies it through pitch and rhythm. When necessary for this process, Monteverdi repeated words and phrases and by this and harmonic means linked the fragments of recitative into coherent arches of melody. Particularly notable is the setting of the last line, "a dio terra" (measures 6–64). Here the rhythmic parallelism, the chromaticism, the rising pitch to the climax on "e sole," and the leap down to a free seventh against the bass convey the depth of Orfeo's grief.

For the first section of the chorus, Monteverdi put the recitative line of the first Pastore (shepherd, measures 28–33), with slight rhythmic modifications, in the bass and built the other four parts on it. As in the *kommos* of the Greek theater, which was a lament by the chorus in dialogue with one or more characters on stage, the chorus joins Orfeo and the shepherds in bemoaning Euridice's death. Then, in the second section (after the double bar), the chorus assumes its usual function, offering moralizing reflections on the stage action. Humankind, it sings, should not trust in the goods and pleasures of the world, for they are elusive and pass quickly. Monteverdi here resorted to the word-painting of the polyphonic madrigal—tenors and basses leap a minor sixth for "a gran salita" (a steep ascent); all the voices speed up for the idea of flight at "che tosto fugge" and leap down sixths at "il precipizio."

CLAUDIO MONTEVERDI

L'incoronazione di Poppea

57

Act I, Scene 3

Tutte le opere di Claudio Monteverdi, ed. G. Francesco Malipiero (© Copyright 1929 by Universal Edition A. G., Vienna), 13:29–35. Copyright renewed. All rights reserved. Used by permission of European American Music Distributors Corp. Sole U.S. Agent for Universal Edition. Vienna.

352

ve _ di an _ zi mai non mi ve _ di   per _ chè

355

s'è ver   che nel tuo cor io   si _ a en _ tra'l tuo

358 (#)

sen cela _ ta non posso non pos_so non pos_so da tuoi lumi es _ ser   mi _ ra _

361

_ta non posso non posso non posso da tuoi lumi es _ ser   mi _ ra _   ta.

366 [5]

NERONE

A _ do _ ra _ ti mie i ra _ i deh resta _ temi ho _ ma _ _ i deh resta _ temi homa _

p

371

_i riman_tio mia Poppe _ a, cor, vezzo, e lu_ce e lu_ce mi _ a.

374 POPPEA

Deh, non dir di par _ tir, che di vo_ce sia_ma _ ra un so_lo accento Ahi

377

pe _ rir, ahi mancar que _ st'al _ ma sen _ _ to.

381 NERONE

Non te _ mer non te _ mer non te _ mer tu stai me_co stai me_co a tutte

386

l'ho _ re splendor negl'occhi e

POPPEA

Signor, deh non partire,	Sir, please don't go.
Sostien, che queste braccia	Allow these arms
Ti circondino il collo,	to encircle your neck,
Come le tue bellezze	as your beauty
Circondano il cor mio,	encircles my heart.

NERO

Poppea, lascia ch'io parta.	Poppea, let me go.

POPPEA

Non partir, Signor, deh non partire	Dont't leave, Sir, please don't go.
Appena spunta l'alba, et tu che sei	The dawn is barely breaking, and you, who are
L'incarnato mio Sole,	my incarnated Sun,
La mia palpabil luce,	my light made palpable,
E l'amoroso dì de la mia vita,	the loving day of my life,
Vuoi sì repente far da me partita!	want to part from me so quickly.
Deh non dir	Please, don't say
Di partir,	that you're leaving.
Che di voce sì amara a un solo accento	It is such a bitter word that from one hint of it,
Ahi, perir, ahi spirar quest'alma io sento.	ah, I feel my soul dying, expiring.

NERO

La nobiltà de nascimenti tuoi	The nobility of your birth
Non permette che Roma	does not permit that Rome
Sappia che siamo uniti.	should know that we are together,
In sin ch'Ottavia non riman' esclusa	until Ottavia is set aside,
Col repudio da me: Vanne, ben mio;	repudiated by me. Go, my dear,
In un sospir, che vien	within a sigh that rises
Dal profondo del cor	from the depths of my heart
Includo un bacio, o cara et un' a Dio,	I enclose a kiss, dearest, and a farewell.
Si rivedrem ben tosto, Idolo mio.	We shall see each other soon, my idol.

POPPEA

Signor, sempre mi vedi,	My lord, you see me constantly;
Anzi mai non mi vedi.	rather, you never see me.
Perchè s'è ver, che nel tuo cor io sia	Because, if it's true that I am in your heart,
Entr' al tuo sen celata	hidden in your breast,
Non posso da' tuoi lumi esser mirata.	I cannot by your eyes be viewed.

NERO

Adorati miei rai,
Deh restate homai
Rimanti, o mia Poppea,
Cor, vezzo, e luce mia.

My adored rays,
please stay, then;
remain, O my Poppea,
my heart, my charm, my light.

POPPEA

Deh non dir. . . .

Please don't say . . .

NERO

Non temer, tu stai meco a tutte l'hore,
Splendor negl'occhi, e deità nel core.

Do not fear; stay with me for all time,
splendor of my eyes, goddess of my heart.

—GIOVANNI FRANCESCO BUSENELLO

Monteverdi wrote this opera in his seventy-fourth year on a libretto by Giovanni Francesco Busenello (1598–1659) for performance in Venice in 1642. The love scene between Nero and Poppea in Act I, Scene 3, passes through various levels of recitative, from speechlike unmeasured passages with few cadences, through a style not unlike the Prologue of *Orfeo*, to measured arioso. The aria passages are similarly varied in their degrees of formal organization and lyricism. Monteverdi sometimes turned to aria style even when the poet did not provide strophic or other closed verse forms.

For example, the composer interrupted Nero's recitative with a short triple-time flowing melody for the half-line "Vanne, ben mio." The poet obviously intended the lines "in un sospir che vien/ dal profondo del cor"—of six syllables each (instead of the usual seven or eleven)—to be set as an aria passage, prompting Monteverdi to state a triple-meter harmonic pattern twice, with a slightly different melody each time. But though Poppea's speech, *Signor, sempre mi vedi,* is in *versi sciolti* (blank verse), Monteverdi chose to set it in a similar way, as a two-strophe variation on a harmonic pattern, this time in duple meter. But the poet's more lyrical speech for Poppea, *Deh non dir,* he set as recitative.

Monteverdi dealt very freely with the libretto's formal structure. Content rather than poetic form, and the urge to heighten emotional expression rather than the desire to charm and dazzle, determined the shifts from recitative to aria and back, and from one level of speech-song to another.

58 Marc' Antonio Cesti (1623–1669)

Orontea: Act II, Scene 17

Intorno all'idol mio

Edited by William Holmes (Wellesley: Wellesley Edition, No. 11, 1973), pp. 158–62.

me___, cor — te — si, cor — te — si au — ret ———— te ————.

7

Al mio ben___ che ri — po — sa Su l'a ———— li___ del ———— la quie-te____ Gra—ti____, gra-ti____ so—gni as-si-ste——te_____, E'l

mio racchiu—so ar—do—re Sve—la—te-li per me__, lar——————ve d'a—

—mo————re____. E'l mio racchiu—so ar—do—re Sve—la—te-li per me__, sve—

6   ♭   ♭

-la————te—li per me——, lar————————————————ve d'a——mo————re————.

ORONTEA

Intorno all'idol mio	Around my idol
Spirate, pur spirate	breathe, just breathe,
Aure soavi e grate	breezes sweet and pleasant,
E nelle guance elette	and on the favored cheeks
Baciatelo per me, cortesi aurette.	kiss him for me, gentle breezes.
Al mio ben che riposa	To my darling, who sleeps
Su l'ali della quiete	on the wings of calm,
Grati sogni assistete,	happy dreams induce;
E'l mio racchiuso ardore	and my covert ardor
Svelateli per me, larve d'amore.	unveil to him, phantoms of love.

—GIACINTO ANDREA CICOGNINI

Cesti's *Orontea*, with a libretto by Giacinto Andrea Cicognini, was first produced in Venice in 1649 and became one of the most frequently performed operas of the mid–1600s both in Italy and abroad.

In the previous scene, Orontea, unmarried queen of Egypt, who has been reluctant to acknowledge her love for the painter Alidoro, discovers him painting a portrait of a rival lady of the court and realizes she is about to lose him. She resolves to marry him; in this aria, as she watches him sleeping, she confesses her love.

Orontea's big scene shows how elaborate the aria had become by mid-century. The two violins play throughout, not merely in ritornellos before and after the singer's strophes. The form is the familiar strophic one, though the music makes some adjustments to the new text of the second strophe. The dimensions are generous, and throughout we hear the new bel canto vocal idiom of smooth, mainly diatonic line and easy rhythms that are grateful to the singer. The expressive leap down of a diminished seventh (measure 23) and the unprepared seventh in the following measure stand out (the passage is heard in the opening ritornello and several more times later).

59 CLAUDIO MONTEVERDI

Madrigal: *Ohimè dov'è il mio ben*

Prima parte

Concerto, Settimo libro de madrigali a 1. 2. 3. 4. & 6. voci, con altri generi de canti (Venice, 1619). *Tutte le opere di Claudio Monteverdi*, ed. G. Francesco Malipiero (© Copyright 1929 by Universal Edition A. G.,Vienna), 12:152–59. Copyright renewed. All rights reserved. Used by permission of European American Music Distributors Corp. Sole U.S.Agent for Universal Edition,Vienna.

Seconda parte

Terza parte

Quarta e ultima parte

Ohimè dov'è il mio ben, dov'è il mio core?
Chi m'asconde il mio ben e chi m'el toglie?
Dunque ha potuto sol desio d'honore
Darmi fera cagion di tante doglie.
Dunque ha potuto in me più che'l mio amore
Ambizios'e troppo lievi voglie.
Ahi sciocco mondo e cieco, ahi cruda sorte
Che ministro mi fai della mia morte.
—BERNARDO TASSO

Alas, where is my love, where is my heart?
Who conceals my treasure and who takes it away?
Thus desire for honor alone was capable
of giving me strong grounds for so many griefs.
Thus more power than my love had my
ambitious and too trifling aspirations.
Ah, stupid world, and blind; ah, cruel fate!
You make me executioner of my own death.

One of the most beautiful compositions in Monteverdi's seventh book of madrigals, published in 1619, is this romanesca for two soprano voices. Here the composer applied both concertato method and the organizing force of the strophic variation. The duetting solo voices, often meeting in dissonant clashes, are brought into harmonious agreement through the ostinato pattern and its basso continuo. In this madrigal, each note of the romanesca ostinato pattern (see example below) usually occupies three measures but is sometimes contracted to two. The pattern consists of a treble melody for singing *ottave rime* (of which this poem is an example) and its characteristic harmonization. In the treble parts Monteverdi preserved the outline of the romanesca melody, while he interpolated passing notes in the basso continuo. This strong structural scaffolding freed the composer to indulge in a variety of artful and expressive devices—canonlike imitation between the voices, moments of recitative, word-descriptive madrigalisms, striking dissonant clashes, and coloratura.

Aria della Romanesca

BARBARA STROZZI (1619–AFTER 1664)

Cantata: *Lagrime mie*

From Barbara Strozzi, *Diporti di Euterpe overo Cantate & ariette a voce sola*, Op. 7 (Venice: Alessandro Magni, 1659), ed. in Carol MacClintock, *The Solo Song 1580–1730* (New York: Norton, 1973), pp. 81–88, corrected by reference to the 1659 edition. Half-brackets indicate colored notation for hemiola

-mè,_____ mi_____ do - nò, Il pa - ter - no ri - gor,_____ il pa - ter - no ri-

-gor _____ l'im-prig-gio-nò. Tra due mu-ra rin-chiu-sa stà la bel-la in-no-

-cen - te Do-ve giun-ger non può rag-gio di so - le, E quel che più mi

duo - le ed ac-cresc' il mio mal, tor-men - ti e pe - ne, È

[Tempo I°] 65

-te! La - - - - - - gri-me

mi - e, à che, à che vi trat-te-ne - te? 70

15

Aria

1. Li-dia, ahi-me, veg-go man - car-mi, Li-dia, ahi-mè, veg-go man-car - mi. L'i-dol
2. Se la mor - te m'è gra - di-ta, se la mor-te m'è gra-di - ta, Or che

75

mio, che tan to a do - - - - ro, Stà co - lei tra du - ri mar-mi per cui
son pri-vo di spe - - - ne, Dhè to - glie-te-mi la vi-ta (Ve ne

spi - ro, per cui spi - ro   E pur_____ non mo - - ro. Stà co-lei tra du-ri
pre-go, ve ne pre - go) a - spre mi e pe - - ne. Dhè to-glie-te-mi la

mar-mi, per cui spi-ro, per cui spi - ro   E pur_____ non mo - - ro.
vi - ta, (ve ne pre-go, ve ne pre - go) a - spre mi e pe - - ne._____

Adagio   90

Ma ben m'ac-cor - go,   che per tor-men-tar - - mi mag - gior - men -

Lagrime mie, à che vi trattenete,	My tears, what holds you back,
Perchè non isfogate il fier' dolore,	why don't you give vent to the fierce pain
Chi mi toglie 'l respiro e opprime il core?	that takes away my breath and weighs on my heart?
Lidia, che tant' adoro,	Lidia, whom I adore so much,
Perchè un guardo pietoso, ahimè, mi donò,	because of the pitying glance, alas, that she gave me,
Il paterno rigor l'impriggionò.	paternal severity has imprisoned her.
Tra due mura rinchiusa	Locked up between two walls,
Stà la bella innocente,	remains the innocent beauty,
Dove giunger non può raggio di sole,	where no ray of sun can reach,
E quel che più mi duole	and what pains me most
Ed accresc'il mio mal, tormenti	and increases my discomfort, torments,
e pene,	and anguish,
È che per mia cagione	is that because of me
Prova male il mio bene.	my beloved suffers.
E voi lumi dolenti, non piangete!	And you, pained eyes, weep not!
Lagrime mie, à che vi trattenete?	Tears, what holds you back?
Lidia, ahimè, veggo mancarmi.	Lidia, alas, I feel myself failing.
L'idol mio, che tanto adoro,	My idol, whom I adore so much
Stà colei tra duri marmi	remains between hard marble walls.
Per cui spiro e pur non moro.	For her I sigh, yet I don't die.
Se la morte m'è gradita,	If death suits me,
Or che son privo di spene,	now that I am deprived of hope,
Dhè, toglietemi la vita	Oh, take away my life—
(Ve ne prego) aspre mie pene.	I beg you—my bitter suffering.
Ma ben m'accorgo, che per tormentarmi	Still I realize that to torment me
Maggiormente, la sorte	the more, destiny
Mi niega anco la morte.	even denies me death.
Se dunqu'è vero, o Dio,	It is true then, O God,
Che sol del pianto mio,	that only for my tears
Il rio destino ha sete.	does cruel fate thirst.

In its form, a succession of sections of recitative, arioso, and aria, this work is representative of the solo cantatas of the mid-seventeenth century. The poet may be Giulio Strozzi (of a Florentine noble family but residing in Venice), with whom Barbara Strozzi lived from childhood and who may have been her father. (She set many of his verses.) He founded an academy, the Unisoni, partly to give her an outlet for her performances and compositions.

Except for two stanzas of four eight-syllable lines each, which Strozzi set as a strophic aria (measures 71–87), the text is made up of madrigal-type verse of seven- and eleven-syllable lines without a regular rhyme scheme. She divided this free verse into sections according to content. The first three lines, in which the poet addresses his tears, she made into a lament. The next ten lines, a narration about Lidia, the object of the poet's love, she set as an arioso. When the poet recalled the weeping eyes (measures 49ff.), the composer invoked the conventional emblem of the lament—the descending bass in triple meter. With the return of the opening line, "Lagrime mie, a che vi trattenete?," Strozzi brought back its music as a kind of refrain. After the Aria (so marked in the original), a short recitative leads to a triple-time bel canto section built on a descending-fourth bass, which is abandoned for two closing sections, the first ending deceptively on G (measure 116), the last on the tonic, E minor.

The dry declamation of theatrical dialogue did not fit such intimate poetic texts, so composers softened, sweetened, and intensified the recitative style in the cantatas meant for chamber performance. In the opening recitative, Strozzi very artfully exploited many of the rhetorical devices that the Roman composers Luigi Rossi (1597–1653) and Giacomo Carissimi (1605–1674) had introduced into cantata recitative. The hesitations on the dissonant D♯, A, and F♯ over the opening E-minor harmony, together with the C♮ of the harmonic-minor scale, make a most moving and vivid projection of the lamenting lover's weeping and sobbing. In the Arioso, the tasteful word-inspired runs at "adoro," "pietoso," and "rigor," the delicate chromaticism at "tormenti," and the compelling seventh chords and suspensions—particularly over the descending basses—show Strozzi's mastery in applying the affective vocabulary of this genre.

61 GIOVANNI GABRIELI (CA. 1553–1612)

Grand Concerto: *In ecclesiis*

Gabrieli, *Symphoniae sacrae* (Venice, 1615). *Opera omnia*, ed. Denis Arnold, vol. 5 (American Institute of Musicology, 1969), pp. 32–55.

In ecclesiis benedicite Domino, Alleluia.
In omni loco dominationis benedic
anima mea Dominum, Alleluia.
In Deo salutari meo et gloria mea,
Deus auxilium meum et spes mea in
Deo est, Alleluia.
Deus noster, te invocamus, te laudamus,
    te adoramus;
libera nos, salva nos, vivifica nos,
Alleluia.
Deus adiutor noster in aeternum, Alleulia.

In churches bless the Lord, Alleluia.
In every place of government, bless
the Lord, O my soul, Alleluia.
In God is my salvation and my glory.
God is my help, and my hope is in
God, Alleluia.
Our God, we implore you, we praise you,
    we worship you;
free us, save us, enliven us,
Alleluia.
God, our helper in eternity, Alleluia.

This work is a magnificent example of the *grand concerto*, a genre that combines vocal soloists with choral and instrumental ensembles. Gabrieli was a master of the medium in which two or more choirs combined and separated in projecting a sacred text. Antiphonal performance by two half-choirs (*cori spezzati*) of psalms of praise was prescribed at St. Mark's in Venice early in the sixteenth century for certain feasts, and Gabrieli dramatically expanded on this tradition.

The brilliant sonorities commanded by Gabrieli come from three groups: four solo voices, which usually perform as an ensemble, though some sing passages alone; a four-part chorus; a six-part instrumental ensemble; and an organ continuo, which plays throughout. At a time when parts were usually issued without designating the instruments, Gabrieli carefully specified the instrumentation: three cornetti, an alto violin (analogous to the modern viola), and two sackbuts. These forces alternately contrast with each other, join in various combinations, or unite in a massive tutti.

The text is not liturgical, although it borrows phrases from liturgical chants. It combines words of praise to God and a plea for help and salvation. The frequent returns of the refrain "Alleluia," which proclaim a mood of jubilation, illustrate the variety of scoring. In the first Alleluia (measures 6–12), the solo soprano and the chorus exchange short motives, then join in a florid affirmation. The following Alleluias have essentially the same music, but the second (measures 25–31) gives the bass the solo role, the third (measures 62–68) features an alto-tenor duet, joined by the instruments as it answers the chorus, and the next (measures 95–101) pits a soprano-bass duet against the chorus. In the final Alleluia (measures 119–29), the chorus, combined with the instruments, contrasts with the entire solo vocal ensemble. Each of these refrains has the same harmonic plan: a succession of major harmonies in a cycle of fifths from F up to A.

As in the Alleluias, Gabrieli built the rest of the composition around short, crisp motives inspired by the rhythm of the text. Ornamental eighth notes that would normally be grouped over one syllable are set to separate syllables, as in "om-ni" (measure 16), "do-mi-na-tio-nis" (measures 17–19),

"De-o est" (measures 54–56), and "in-vo-ca-mus" (measures 72–73). This exaggeration of weak syllables makes the motives stand out and imprints them on the memory.

Gabrieli indulged in some daring harmonies, not so much for the sake of text expression as for their brilliant colors—for example, the cornetto's strident *F* in the Sinfonia (measure 31), and the repeated cross-relations at "in Deo salutari meo" (measures 42, 45), caused by the shift from the major chord on *E* to that on *C*. This same major-third relationship punctuates the entrance of the Alleluias, which break in suddenly with F major after a cadence on *A*.

62 LODOVICO VIADANA (CA. 1560–1627)
Sacred Concerto: *O Domine, Jesu Christe*

O Do - mi - ne Je - su Chri - ste

Je - su Chri - ste, pa - stor bo - ne,

ju - stos con - ser - va, pec - ca - to - res ju - sti - fi -

ca, om - ni - bus fi - de - li - bus om - ni - bus fi -

Reprinted by permission of Bärenreiter-Verlag, Kassel, Basel, Tours, and London, from: *Cento concerti ecclesiastici opera duodecima* (Venice, 1602), ed. Claudio Gallico (Kassel, etc., 1964), pp. 64–65.

O Domine Jesu Christe,
pastor bone,
justos conserva
peccatores justifica,
omnibus fidelibus miserere,
et propitius esto mihi misero
et indigno peccatori. Amen.

O Lord Jesus Christ,
good shepherd,
preserve the righteous,
do justice to the sinners,
have mercy on all the faithful,
and be gracious toward me, wretched
and unworthy sinner. Amen.

In this concerto from the 1602 collection, Viadana created the illusion of a complex texture in a single voice by having it imitate itself at different pitch levels. This reduction of the polyphonic idiom was of great practical significance: it allowed a work to be performed, if necessary, by one singer or a small number of them. Instead of doubling or replacing vocal parts by instruments, as had been done in the sixteenth century, the thoroughbass and the chords improvised on it took the place of the other parts.

The term *concerto* applies to this work because it concerts (unites) a voice and instrumental accompaniment. Other concertos in Viadana's 1602 collection are for two, three, or four singers with thorough bass. All of them belong to the category of concertos for few voices as opposed to the grand concerto.

In style this piece is closer to the madrigals of Caccini than it is to recitative. The chromatic line at "mihi misero" (measures 29–30) is especially madrigalistic. Like Gabrieli, Viadana used the shift from E major to C major for harmonic color and as a mark of punctuation (measures 6–7, 15–16, 19).

Alessandro Grandi (ca. 1575–1630)

Motet: *O quam tu pulchra es*

63

Values halved in triple meter. *Ghirlanda sacra. Libro primo . . . per Leonardo Simonetti* (Venice, 1625). Rudolf Werhart, ed., in *Drei Hohelied Motetten*. Cantio sacra, no. 23 (Cologne: Verlag Edmund Bieler, 1960), pp. 7–9. Reprinted by permission.

O quam tu pulchra es, amica mea,
quam pulchra es, columba mea,
o quam tu pulchra es, formosa mea.
Oculi tui columbarum,
capilli tui sicut greges caprarum
et dentes tui sicut greges tonsarum.
O quam tu pulchra es.
Veni de Libano, amica mea,
columba mea, formosa mea.
O quam tu pulchra es,
veni, coronaberis.
Surge, surge, propera, sponsa mea,
surge, dilecta mea,
surge, immaculata mea.
Quia amore langueo.
Surge, veni, quia amore langueo.
—*Song of Songs*, 4:1, 4:8

O how fair you are, my love,
how fair you are, my dove,
how fair you are, my beauty.
Your eyes, the eyes of doves,
your hair, like a flock of goats,
and your teeth like a flock of sheep newly shorn.
O how fair you are.
Come with me from Lebanon, my love,
my dove, my beauty.
O how fair you are,
come, you will make a garland.
Arise, hasten, my bride,
arise, my delight,
arise, my spotless one.
For I pine of love. Arise,
come, for I pine of love.

On a text from the *Song of Songs,* a source popular for musical setting at this time, this solo motet of around 1625 shows how a composer could, without breaking stride, incorporate into a single composition elements from recitative, solo madrigal, and bel canto aria. The first twenty-one measures are clearly recitative, but of a more melodious, rhythmic kind than that used in the theater. Marco Scacchi called it "hybrid recitative" (*recitativo inbastardito*), a mixed style found more appropriate for the church. Then there is a passage in triple-time aria style (measures 22 to 34). It is interrupted by five measures of recitative that recall the opening. After a continuation of the aria, the rest of the motet is in the recitative style. Grandi took advantage of the frequent recurrence of the words "O quam tu pulchra es" to bring back the opening music as a kind of refrain.

Giacomo Carissimi (1605–1674)

Historia di Jephte

a) Filia: *Plorate colles*

Edited by Gottfried Wolters, figured bass realized by Mathias Siedel (Wolfenbüttel: Möseler Verlag, 1969), pp. 29–39. Reprinted by permission.

me - am et Jeph - te fi - li-am u - ni - ge - ni-tam in car - mi-ne do -

lo - ris la - men - ta - - - mi - ni, et

Jeph - te fi - li-am u - ni - ge - ni-tam in car - mi - ne do -

lo - ris la - men - ta - - mi - ni.

DAUGHTER

Plorate colles, dolete montes
et in afflictione cordis mei ululate!
Ecce moriar virgo
et non potero morte mea
meis filiis consolari,
ingemiscite silvae, fontes et flumina,
in interitu virginis lachrimate,
fontes et flumina.

Heu me dolentem in laetitia populi,
in victoria Israel et gloria patris mei,
ego sine filiis virgo,
ego filia unigenita moriar et non vivam.
Exhorrescite rupes, obstupescite colles,
valles et cavernae in sonitu horribili resonate!
Plorate, filii Israel,
plorate virginitatem meam
et Jephte filiam unigenitam in carmine doloris
lamentamini.

Weep, hills, grieve, mountains
and in the affliction of my heart, wail!
Suddenly I shall die a virgin
and I shall not be able at my death
to be consoled by my children.
Groan, forests, springs, and rivers.
Weep for the death of a virgin,
springs and rivers.

Woe is me, sorrowful, amidst the people's joy
in Israel's victory and my country's glory.
I, without children, a virgin,
I, an only daughter, will die and not live.
Shudder, crags; be stupefied, hills;
valleys and caves, echo the horrible sound.
Weep, sons of Israel,
bewail my virginity
and lament Jephte's only daughter
in songs of sorrow.

b) Chorus: *Plorate filii Israel*

CHORUS

Plorate filii Israel, plorate omnes virgines
et filiam Jephte unigenitam in carmine doloris
lamentamini.

Weep, sons of Israel; weep all virgins,
and lament Jephthe's only daughter
in songs of sorrow.

In this scene, based on Judges 11:29–38, Jephtha, the military leader of the
Israelites, has just returned victorious from a battle. He owes the victory to a
promise he made to the Lord that if allowed to beat the Ammonites, he
would on his return home sacrifice the first person who comes out of his
house. It is his daughter who runs out to meet him with timbrels and
dances.

The daughter's lament, the words of which are not in the biblical
account, is a long, affecting recitative, sweetened, as was customary in the
sacred hybrid style, with arioso passages built on sequences and with
moments of florid song. Two sopranos, representing her companions, echo
some of the daughter's cadential phrases.

Carissimi's recitative introduces expressive dissonances in a way that
recalls the Florentine style, but they exist in a more harmonically determined environment. For example, the soprano's *D* in measure 295 is not
simply a free dissonance but a member of a chord. Even more characteristic

is the *F♯* of measure 302, which is part of a *D* chord over a *G* pedal. Similarly the skip to the seventh in measures 308–09 and the "Neapolitan" lowered sixth at measure 310 and again at measure 314 are harmonic rather than melodic effects. Equally striking are the double suspensions in the chorus (measures 380 ff.). These passages demonstrate how much the emotional intensity of this scene owes to harmonic rather than melodic means.

The excerpt (and the work) closes with a magnificent six-voice chorus of lamentation (b) that employs both polychoral and madrigalistic effects. In what becomes an emblem of lament in the seventeenth century, the choral basses and the basso continuo three times descend a fourth by step (measures 358–70).

65 Heinrich Schütz (1585–1672)

Grand Concerto: *Saul, was verfolgst du mich,*
swv 415

Symphoniarum sacrarum tertia pars, worinnen zubefinden sind deutsche Concerten, Op. 12 (Dresden, 1650), No. 18, ed. Günter Graulich and Paul Horn, Stuttgarter Schützausgabe (Stuttgart: Hänssler-Verlag, 1969), pp. 63–73.

For this composition Schütz chose one of the most dramatic episodes in the New Testament, Paul's description of how he was converted to Christianity (Acts 26:12–14, Revised Standard Version):

> Thus I journeyed to Damascus with the authority and commission of the chief priests. At midday, O king, I saw on the way a light from heaven, brighter than the sun, shining round me and those who journeyed with me. And when we had all fallen to the ground, I heard a voice saying to me in the Hebrew language, "Saul, Saul, why do you persecute me? It hurts you to kick against the goads."

Saul, a Jew, had been sent to Damascus to fetch Christian prisoners. The voice he heard in the desert was that of Christ. The experience led to Saul's conversion and to his career (under the name Paul) as a crusader for Christianity.

The concerto is set for six solo voices (the ensemble Schütz called *favoriti*), two violins, two four-voice choirs, and, it may be assumed, an orchestra that doubles the choral parts. Two-note chords from the D-minor triad rise from the depths of the solo basses through the tenors; then the same music is heard shifting to A minor in the sopranos, and finally the violins return it to D minor. Christ's question "Was verfolgst du mich?" (Why do you persecute me?) is a mesh of dissonant anticipations and suspensions.

So far the medium has been that of the concerto for few voices. Now the grand concerto takes over the same music in a bright D major (measure 17), and the choruses and soloists together reverberate with echoes, suggesting the effect of Christ's voice bouncing off rocky projections in the desert. As the voice rings obsessively in Saul's ear, sections in recitative and arioso for solo voices alternate with the "Saul, Saul" grand-concerto music as a refrain.

The idea of the rising chords may have been suggested to Schütz by Monteverdi's famous madrigal *Hor che'l ciel e la terra*, which contains a similar progression. Schütz worked with Monteverdi and Grandi during a visit to Venice in 1628 and 1629. During previous visits, in 1609 and 1612, he had studied with Giovanni Gabrieli, whose polychoral practice is also reflected here.

66 ENNEMOND GAULTIER (CA. 1575–1651)

Gigue: *La Poste*

a) Lute

Special signs ⌐')*pincé* (mordent with lower auxiliary); ⌐ *coulé* (upward double appoggiatura); ♪,⌐*port de voix* (appoggiatura starting on lower auxiliary). *Oeuvres du vieux Gaultier*, André Souris, ed. (Paris: Editions du CNRS, 1966). Nos. 63, 85, pp. 83, 111.

b) Arrangement for harpsichord by Jean-Henri D'Anglebert

These two examples illustrate the transfer of the lute idiom to the harpsi-chord. Although the latter instrument, unlike the lute, is capable of playing chords as simultaneities, the arranger has deferred to the limitations of the lute and distributed the component notes of a chord over several beats in *style brisé* (broken style). The ornaments tend to fall on the same notes and beats in both arrangements, and their function is similar: to mark certain beats as a drum might do, to promote continuity, to play down certain other beats, or to intensify dissonance and thereby the harmonic motion.

This gigue, in duple meter, is in the common binary form, with a close on the dominant in the first part, on the tonic in the second.

67 JOHANN JAKOB FROBERGER (1616–1667)

Lamentation faite sur la mort très douloureuse de Sa Majesté Impériale
Ferdinand le troisième et se joüe lentement avec discretion

Oeuvres complètes pour clavecin, ed. Howard Schott (Paris: Heugel, HE.33.702), Le Pupitre 58, pp. 160–61.

Froberger, in his toccatas, betrayed the influence of his teacher Frescobaldi, but this piece demonstrates his mastery of the French clavecin style. It is in the genre of the *tombeau*, which French lutenists and harpsichordists customarily wrote upon the death of one of their colleagues. Froberger composed this tombeau ("Lamentation on the very sad death of His Imperial Majesty Ferdinand III, to be played slowly, with circumspection") in 1657 to mourn the death of the emperor whose court in Vienna he served as organist. In keeping with the French tradition, this piece is a slow allemande, but its hesitations and impulsive runs remove it from the dance. The *style brisé*, through which Froberger was one of the first to imitate lute music on the harpsichord, dominates the texture. Both the rare key of F minor and the prominent threefold *F*s at the end allude to the emperor's name. Another programmatic touch is the arpeggio in the final two measures from deep in the bass to the treble, representing the ascent of the emperor's soul.

GIROLAMO FRESCOBALDI (1583–1643)

Toccata No. 3 (1637)

Toccata Terza

Toccate d'intavolatura di cimbalo et organo libro 1 (Rome, 1637; first published in *Il primo libro d'intavolatura di toccate di cimbalo et organo*, 1628), ed. Pierre Pidoux, Orgel- und Klavierwerke, vol. 3 (Kassel: Bärenreiter-Verlag, 1954), pp. 11–13.

The restless character of this toccata, meant to be played before a Mass, is typical of Frescobaldi's works. The music is constantly approaching a cadence on either the dominant or tonic, but until the very end the composer evaded or weakened the goal harmonically, rhythmically, or through continued part-movement. Some of the notable points of arrival and immediate departure are measures 5 (dominant), 8 (dominant minor), and 13 (tonic major), and measures 17, 26, and 31 (all tonic minor). The restlessness is also felt in the shifting of styles. At the outset the toccata breathes the spirit of recitative, with jagged lines and nervous rhythms. At measure 5 a short arioso passage, with chains of suspensions over a walking bass, leads to an imitative section (measures 8–11). In the remainder of the piece the two hands alternate, one playing scales and turns while the other has chords, or they toss back and forth short figures that lie easily under the fingers. The emphasis on the dominant and tonic strongly sets the keynote for what is to follow in the music of the Mass.

ALESSANDRO SCARLATTI (1660–1725)

La Griselda

69

Act II, Scene 1: *Mi rivedi*

Reprinted by permission of the publishers from *The Operas of Alessandro Scarlatti*, Vol. III: *Griselda,* Donald J. Grout and Elizabeth B. Hughes, eds. (Harvard Publications in Music, 8). Cambridge, Mass.: Harvard University Press, ©1975 by the President and Fellows of Harvard College.

Mi ri - ve - di o sel - va om-bro - sa,   ma non più Re-gi-na e spo - sa,   mi ri-

ve - di sven-tu-ra - ta,   mi ri - ve-di sven - tu-ra - ta, di-sprez-za-ta, di-sprez-za-ta pa-sto-rel - la,   sven-tu-

ra - ta,   di-sprez-za - ta pa-sto-rel - la.

È pur quel - lo, quel - lo, quel - lo il pa - trio mon - te, que-sta è pur l'a - mi - ca

fon - te, quel-lo è il pra - to e il que-sto è il ri - o; e sol i - o, e sol io non son, no, no, non son più quel -

la no, non son più quel - la no, non son più, no, non son più quel - la ————. Mi ri -

Dal segno

GRISELDA

Mi rivedi o selva ombrosa,	You see me again, o shady forest,
Ma non più Regina e sposa,	but no longer queen and bride;
Sventurata, disprezzata	unfortunate, disdained,
Pastorella.	a shepherdess.
È pur quello il patrio monte,	Yet there is my homeland's mountain
Questa è pur l'amica fonte,	and here is still the friendly fountain;
Quello è il prato e questo è il rio;	there is the meadow and this is the river;
E sol io non son più quella.	and only I am not the same.

　　　—Based on the libretto by Apostolo Zeno

La Griselda was first performed in Rome in 1721. In this aria, "You see me again, o shady forest," Griselda expresses conflicting reactions to her situation: a queen for fifteen years, she has been repudiated by King Gualtiero of Sicily. She must return to her humble origins and, besides, serve as maid to the new queen, all this to test her virtue. She addresses the familiar surroundings of her native countryside with a mixture of humiliation and nostalgia.

The mood of subjection is summed up in the melody of the first line, out of which the rest of the main (A) section develops through extension, sequence, and combinatorial methods. The subordinate (B) section, linked to the A section rhythmically, for a moment presents the bright side, her pleasure at being home. Only the vocal portion of the A section is then repeated (*da capo dal segno*).

This aria is a concise example of the abbreviated format, popular in the 1720s, in which the opening ritornello is omitted in the da capo. The scheme is:

Section:	Ritornello	A	Transitional Rit	B		A
Key:	C minor			Modulation to E♭		C minor
Measure:	1	4	16	18	19	26 (27=)4—18

The ritornello and the A section occupy 18 measures, all in C minor except for a brief foray into B♭ major. The B section, of 8 measures, modulates from the C-minor cadence at the end of the transitional ritornello by way of G minor to E♭. Then, skipping over the opening ritornello, the singer returns to the A section directly, closing the aria at the fermata that ends the transitional ritornello.

JEAN-BAPTISTE LULLY (1632–1687)
Armide

a) Ouverture

Edited by Robert Eitner, *Publikationen älterer praktischer und theoretischer Musikwerke*, 14 (Leipzig: Breitkopf & Härtel, 1885) pp. 1–3, 100–04.

b) Act II, Scene 5: Armide: *Enfin il est en ma puissance*

-té de lui ra-vir le jour! A ce jeu-ne hé-ros tout cè-de sur la ter-re. Qui croi-

-rait qu'il fut ne seu-le-ment pour la guer-re? Il sem-ble e-tre fait pour l'a-mour.

Ne puis-je me ven-ger à moins qu'il ne pé-ris-se? Hé! ne suf-fit-il

pas que l'a-mour le pu-nis-se? Puis-qu'il n'a pu trou-ver mes yeux as-sez char-

* On the recording, the music returns to measure 71, continues through measure 90, and again repeats measures 86–90.

ARMIDE

Enfin il est en ma puissance,
Ce fatal ennemi, ce superbe vainqueur.
Le charme du sommeille livre à ma vengeance;
Je vais percer son invincible coeur.
Par lui tous mes captifs sont sortis
    d'esclavage;
Qu'il éprouve toute ma rage.
Quel trouble me saisit? qui me fait hésiter?
Qu'est-ce qu'en sa faveur le pitié me veut dire?
Frappons . . . Ciel! qui peut m'arrêter?
Achevons . . . je frémis! vengeons–nous
    . . . je soupire!
Est-ce ainsi que je dois me venger aujourd'hui?
Ma colère s'éteint quand j'approche de lui.
Plus je le voi, plus ma vengeance est vaine;

Mon bras tremblant se refuse à ma haine.
Ah! quelle cruauté de lui ravir le jour!
A ce jeune héros tout cède sur la terre.
Qui croirait qu'il fut né seulement pour la guerre?
Il semble être fait pour l'Amour.
Ne puis-je me venger à moins qu'il ne périsse?
Hé! ne suffit-il pas que l'amour le punisse?
Puisqu'il n'a pu trouver mes yeux assez charmants,
Qu'il m'aime au moins par mes enchantements.
Que, s'il se peut, je le haïsse.

Venez, venez, seconder mes désirs,
Démons, transformez-vous en d'aimables zéphirs.
Je cède à ce vainqueur, la pitié me surmonte.
Cachez ma foiblesse et ma honte
Dans les plus reculés déserts.
Volez, volez, conduisez-nous au bout de l'univers.
    —PHILIPPE QUINAULT

Finally he is in my power,
  this fatal enemy, this superb warrior.
The charm of sleep delivers him to my vengeance;
  I will pierce his invincible heart.
Through him all my captives have escaped
    from slavery.
Let him feel all my anger.
What fear grips me? what makes me hesitate?
What in his favor does pity want to tell me?
Let us strike . . . Heavens! Who can stop me?
Let us get on with it . . . I tremble! Let us avenge
    . . . I sigh!
Is it thus that I must avenge myself today?
My rage is extinguished when I approach him.
The more I see of him, the more my
    vengeance is ineffectual.
My trembling arm denies my hate.
Ah! What cruelty, to rob him of the light of day!
To this young hero everything on earth surrenders.
Who would believe that he was born only for war?
He seems to be made for love.
Could I not avenge myself unless he dies?
Oh, is it not enough that Love should punish him?
Since he could not find my eyes charming enough,
  let him love me at least through my sorcery,
  so that, if it's possible, I may hate him.

Come, come support my desires,
  demons; transform yourselves into friendly zephyrs.
I give in to this conqueror; pity overwhelms me.
Conceal my weakness and my shame
  in the most remote desert.
Fly, fly, lead us to the end of the universe.

Armide, on a libretto by Philippe Quinault, was one of Lully's last operas, produced in Paris in 1686. The Ouverture, in the form and genre known as the *French overture,* is in two parts. The first is homophonic, slow, and majestic, marked by persistent dotted rhythms and by figures rushing toward the downbeats. Moreover, a French performance convention of the time encouraged "double-dotting," the reading of singly dotted quarter notes as if doubly dotted, and performing even eighth notes as if they were dotted eighth notes. The faster second section, in a compound triple measure, starts with a semblance of fugal imitation. Then the slow tempo returns, together with some reminiscences of the opening music. Each of the two sections is marked with a repeat, in keeping with the overture's dance pedigree: it was originally an allemande. Some later opera overtures and other instrumental pieces began in this way, then continued with a number of additional movements. The orchestra consists entirely of strings, divided into five parts rather than the four that became standard later.

The first part of this monologue is one of the most impressive scenes of recitative in all of Lully's work. Armide is an enchantress who captures knights of the Crusades, casts a spell over them, and holds them for her pleasure in her palace. But against her will she has fallen in love with Renaud, who had incited her anger by freeing her captives. In this scene she aims to slay him as he sleeps. Her dagger ready, she is prevented by her love from plunging it into his breast.

The orchestra introduces the scene with a tense prelude that has the character of the slow section of a French overture. Armide, accompanied by continuo, then sings in an unmetrical rhythm notated in mixed duple and triple measures. This device permits the two accented syllables normally found in each poetic line to fall on downbeats. All the lines, and sometimes caesuras within a line, are marked by rests. Rests are also used dramatically, as in the passage where Armide hesitates: "Let's get it done . . . I tremble . . . let us avenge ourselves . . . I sigh!" (measures 38–42).

Despite the lack of regular meter, Lully's recitative is more melodious than its Italian counterpart, and the line is driven by a more active harmonic background.

The air that follows is accompanied by the orchestra and has the graceful rhythm of a minuet. Armide calls on her demons to transform themselves into zephyrs and transport her and Renaud to some remote desert, where her shame and weakness would not be observed.

HENRY PURCELL (1659–1695)

Dido and Aeneas

Act III, Scene 2

Ground bass

Dido: *Thy hand, Belinda / When I am laid in earth*

Extract of Purcell's *Dido and Aeneas* (Margaret Laurie and Thurston Dart, eds.) reproduced from Purcell Society Edition, Vol. 3.

Chorus: *With drooping wings*

droop - ing wings, with droop - ing wings ye Cu-pids come, And

Cu - pids come, with droop - ing wings ye Cu - pids come, And

droop-ing wings,with droop-ing wings,with droop-ing wings,with droop-ing wings ye Cu-pids come,

with droop - ing wings ye Cu-pids come,_____ ye Cu-pids come,

scat - ter ro - ses, scat-ter, scat-ter_ ro-ses on_her tomb,

scat - ter ro - ses, scat-ter, scat-ter_ ro - ses on her tomb, Soft, soft____ and

And scat-ter, scat-ter_ ro-ses on her tomb, Soft, soft,_

And scat - ter_ ro - ses, scat-ter_ ro-ses_ on her tomb,

[*pp*]

never, never,   nev-er part, and nev-er, never,   nev-er, nev-er part. With droop- part.

never, never,   nev-er part, and nev-er, never,   nev-   er, nev-er part.   part.

never, never,   nev-er part, and nev-er, never,   nev-   er, nev-er part.   With   part.

never, nev-er,   nev-er part, and nev-er, never,   nev-   er, nev-er part.   part.

Purcell wrote this opera on a libretto by Nahum Tate; it was first performed in 1689 by the pupils at a girl's boarding school in Chelsea, a suburb of London, with a few outsiders probably pressed into service for the men's parts. The plot is distantly descended from the fourth book of Vergil's *Aeneid.* A more immediate antecedent is John Blow's court masque *Venus and Adonis,* with which it shares many musical and dramatic features.

Dido's lament *When I am laid in earth* in the last scene is one of the landmarks of seventeenth-century music, a perfect adaptation of technique to expression. The preceding recitative does more than serve as a vehicle for the text; by its slow stepwise descent of a seventh, it portrays the dying Dido and thus prepares us for the lament. But it does not tell us that she is dying because in the midst of an intense love affair with Aeneas she feels abandoned, betrayed, and forlorn when he is called away to resume fighting in the Trojan War.

Purcell followed an Italian opera tradition of setting such laments over a *basso ostinato,* or ground bass. The bass itself grows out of the descending fourth common in such pieces, but it is extended by a two-measure cadence formula, adding up to a five-measure pattern, which is heard ten times. Purcell created great tension and forward thrust by re-attacking suspended notes on the strong beat, intensifying the dissonance. We feel a further jolt when, several times, the dissonance is resolved by skip (for example, at the word "trouble," measures 12 and 13). The violins contribute to the grieving effect by adding their own suspensions and other dissonances.

The closing chorus *With drooping wings* was certainly suggested to Purcell by the final chorus of Blow's *Venus and Adonis*. Equally perfect in workmanship, it is on a larger scale and conveys a more profound depth of sorrow. Descending minor-scale figures portray the cupids' "drooping wings," and arresting pauses mark the words "never part."

HENRY PURCELL

The Fairy Queen

Hark! the ech'ing air a triumph sings

Text by Elkanah Settle (?) from Shakespeare's *A Midsummer Night's Dream*. Reprinted by Broude Bros. (New York, 19–), pp. 179–82.

Several of the airs that Purcell composed for the masque *The Fairy Queen* (1692), a semi-opera adapted from Shakespeare's *A Midsummer Night's Dream*, are modeled on Italian aria types. The motto aria with trumpet obbligato is called on to evoke the ideas of echo and triumph. The voice echoes the trumpet's triumphant flourish but is interrupted by the bass, which in turn echoes the voice. Then, in the manner of the motto aria, the voice begins again, this time continuing with imitations of trumpet fanfares and trills. The second section introduces new themes to illustrate the words "around," "pleased," and "clap," the last a sound-imitation. It is significant that Purcell did not bring back the first section as in the da capo aria, probably because his aria was modeled on the ABB form popular in Italy earlier in the century.

73 DIETRICH BUXTEHUDE (CA. 1637–1707)
Praeludium in E Major, BuxWV 141

Improvisatory

Dietrich Buxtehude, *Sämtliche Orgelwerke*, ed. Josef Hedar (Copenhagen: Wilhelm Hansen Nr. 3922), 2:79–84.

This toccata, like most of Buxtehude's, is designated in the manuscripts simply as "Praeludium;" it contains four fugal sections, each preceded by free
figurative exordia or transitions. The longest free section is the first; the
internal ones are transitional. The piece begins with a three-measure flourish in the right hand, a grand upbeat to the first E-major chord, which is the
goal also of the eight-measure harmonic exploration that follows. The first
fugue (measure 13ff.) has two full expositions in the four voices, in
Buxtehude's favorite order of soprano, alto, tenor, bass. After an episode built
on the tail of the subject that modulates to the dominant, there is a further,
incomplete exposition (measure 36ff.). The free section that ensues is full of
exuberant runs that take the pitch to the highest point in the piece; it features two "long trills"—so marked in the score—in the pedal part (measures
51 and 53). The second fugal section, marked Presto, breaks up into imitations of a short figure after only two entries; by means of a brief suspenseful
transition it reaffirms the tonic for an informal three-voice fugue without
pedal in $\frac{12}{8}$ gigue-time (measures 75–86) on a subject that is derived from the
first one. A transitional Adagio leads to the final, quite formal exposition of
another subject derived from the first. The form of the piece may be sum-
marized as follows:

$\frac{4}{4}$				$\frac{12}{8}$	$\frac{4}{4}$		
Free	Fugue	Free	Fugal/Figurative	Fugal	Trans.	Fugue	Coda
1	13	47	60	75	87	91	104	110

74 DIETRICH BUXTEHUDE
Chorale Prelude: *Danket dem Herrn*, BuxWV 181

Dietrich Buxtehudes Werke für Orgel, ed. Phillip Spitta, *Neue Ausgabe* von Max Seiffert, 2 (Leipzig, 1904), pp. 1–2.

This setting of "Thank the Lord, for He is very kind" treats the chorale as a cantus firmus, but in each variation the chorale melody appears in a different voice: in the top part in the first variation, in the pedal as a middle voice in the second, and in the pedal as a bass in the third and last. For each statement of the chorale Buxtehude invented a new, highly individualized subject that was developed initially by imitation, then through free counterpoint.

75 FRANÇOIS COUPERIN (1668–1733)

Vingt-cinquième ordre

a) *La Visionaire*

For a guide to the realization of Couperin's ornaments, see HWM, 5th ed., pp. 370–71. *Pièces de clavecin, quatrième livre*, ed. Kenneth Gilbert. ©1970 Heugel et Cie. Reprinted by permission. Theodore Presser Company, sole representative U.S.A.

b) *La Misterieuse*

c) *La Monflambert*

17

Tendrement, sans lenteur

d) *La Muse victorieuse*

18

Audacieusement

e) *Les Ombres errantes*

19

Languissamment

François Couperin published twenty-seven *ordres*, or groups of pieces, for harpsichord between 1713 and 1730. This set, the twenty-fifth, appeared in 1730 in the fourth book, along with seven others. The ordres were made up mostly of stylized dances in binary form, like the suites written by German composers, but the dances did not follow any particular sequence. Couperin gave the numbers fanciful and suggestive titles, such as those in this ordre: *La Visionaire* (The Dreamer), *La Misterieuse* (The Mysterious One), *La Monflambert* (a gigue, probably named after Anne Darboulin, who married Monflambert, the king's wine merchant, in 1726), *La Muse victorieuse* (The Victorious Muse), and *Les Ombres errantes* (The Roving Shadows).

La Visionaire, the first movement of this ordre, is a rather whimsical French overture. After reaching the dominant in measure 13, the first half passes into the dominant minor for a moment's meditation. The second half, after a few imitations between the two hands—a passing bow to the obligatory fugue—lapses into an allemande, haunted by memories of the majestic first half.

La Misterieuse, in C major, is a more proper allemande in $\frac{4}{4}$, mainly with steady sixteenth-note motion. It has the typical binary dance form, the first half modulating to the dominant by way of a pedal point on *D* that imitates the sound of a musette, or French bagpipe, and ending in a full cadence on G major. The second section, somewhat longer than the first, touches on some related keys—E minor and A minor. A return to the dominant is made in the bass through half steps down a fifth from *A* to *D* (measures 17–19), while the upper voices pass through some strained harmonies that may well have suggested the title.

La Monflambert is a gigue in $\frac{6}{8}$, and, like the final piece of the ordre, in minor. It must have been a favorite of the person after whom it was named, for these pieces were intended for amateurs to amuse themselves at the harpsichord. It is made up entirely of four-measure phrases. After the second part is played for the second time, the last four bars are repeated as a coda.

La Muse victorieuse displays a formal device characteristic of binary movements of Couperin and, later, Domenico Scarlatti: the last eleven measures of the first half are paralleled in the close of the second half, except that in the former the progression is to the dominant, while in the latter it is from the dominant to the tonic.

Les Ombres errantes may owe its title to the syncopated middle voice, which seems to shadow the top voice erratically, forming chains of suspensions, some of which resolve upward. Marked *languissamment,* this piece, as well as *La Misterieuse,* combines restrained emotionalism with controlling harmonic and melodic logic, exhibiting the sentimental elegance so appealing to the courtiers and amateurs of this age.

76 GIOVANNI LEGRENZI (1626–1690)

Trio Sonata: *La Raspona*

Sonate a due, a tre di Giovanni Legrenzi, Libro primo, Opera seconda (Venice, 1665). Reprinted by permission of Bärenreiter-Verlag, Kassel, Basel, Tours, and London, from *Hortus Musicus* No. 31, Werner Danckert, ed. (Kassel, 1949), pp. 3–7.

21

ADAGGIO

This sonata for two violins and basso continuo (harpsichord and viola da gamba or cello) shows off Legrenzi's renowned aptitude for inventing rhythmically and melodically incisive fugal subjects. The two movements, marked Allegro and "Adaggio," both immediately repeated, have a canzona-like structure in which only the two upper parts are involved in the statements and answers, the bass serving throughout as a foundation.

The Allegro is in two main sections: the first proceeds from G major to C major (measures 1–22); the second returns to G major (measures 22–43). The first section has a series of fugal entries on variants of a single theme. At the outset, the subject is answered at the unison. Then a variation of the subject is heard on the subdominant, answered on the tonic, and again on the dominant, leading to a cadence on the tonic (measure 11). The original subject is now stated in the tonic and answered in the subdominant, followed by an elaboration of the second part of the subject and scalar flourishes that complete the modulation to the subdominant. The second section, in triple time, begins with the two violins exchanging short cantabile motives, but once the dominant of the original key is reached (measure 32), a new fugal subject is briefly exposed.

The Adaggio, after a transitional opening that establishes C major, modulates by means of sequences to the sixth degree (measure 53), when the violins begin to exchange subjects and figurations displaying the verve and agility of the instrument and its player.

77 ARCANGELO CORELLI (1653–1713)
Trio Sonata, Op. 3, No. 2

From *Sonate a tre* (Bologna, 1689). *Les Oeuvres de Arcangelo Corelli,* J. Joachim and F. Chrysander, eds. (London, n.d.), pp. 130–35.

This sonata da chiesa (church sonata) has the typical slow-fast-slow-fast succession of movements. Although the movements, as befits church music, avoid obvious secular connotations, they betray a kinship with the stylized dances of the suite: the first movement with the allemande, the third with the sarabande, and the fourth with the gigue.

Grave, the marking on the first movement, is not merely a designation of tempo but a description of the music's character: serious, intense, and profound. The intensity is expressed by the determined march of the bass and the deliberate suspended dissonance on nearly every downbeat. That dissonance was by then defined as an alien note against a consonant chord is evident in the leaps within chord tones against the dissonance, as in measure 14. Another indication is the ornamental pattern of leaping from a suspension down to a chord tone, then up to the note of resolution (as in measure 15, and in the first Allegro, measures 47–48). Especially typical of Corelli's slow movements are the chains of suspensions that begin in measure 6 while the violins meet, cross, and separate as the bass walks on.

Unlike Legrenzi, Corelli gave the bass in the fast movements an equal share in the fugal action. Indeed the bass is the first to answer the Allegro movement's subject in direct motion, the second violin having answered by inversion and incompletely. After the first exposition only the second part of the subject reappears (measures 36ff.), both in direct motion and inversion. The three notes that are the head of the subject keep intervening as counterpoints. The key of D major is neatly circumscribed by well-prepared cadences in A major, B minor, and E major, before the return to D. This movement is remarkably taut in its exclusion of non-thematic material.

The Adagio resembles a passionate vocal duet in which two singers alternately imitate each other or proceed in parallel motion. The sigh effects in measures 14–15 are operatic, while syncopations and suspensions on the first and second beats of the triple-time measures emphasize through both resolution and dissonance the second beat of the sarabande rhythm. The dance character is reinforced by the hemiola passages (measures 19–21 and 36–39). A Phrygian cadence at the end of the Adagio makes one expect a return to B minor, but instead an Allegro in D major ensues.

The final movement, although a gigue, is simply labeled Allegro. It again involves all three instrumental parts in a fugue, and the subject of the second half is an inversion of that of the first half, as it is in many later gigues for keyboard. There are two sequential episodes of the kind found in later fugues (measures 8–10 and 28–32). Fascination with contrapuntal devices such as inversion, stretto (measures 32–35), and pedal point (measures 15–18) betray the influence of the Bologna school, in which such artifices were cultivated and where Corelli was trained.

Antonio Vivaldi (1678–1741)
Concerto Grosso in G Minor, Op. 3, No. 2, RV 578

a) Adagio e spiccato (first movement)

Vivaldi, *L'estro armonico*, Op. 3 (Amsterdam, 1711), ed. Gian Francesco Malipiero (Milan: Ricordi, 1965), 407:1–33. F. IV, no. 8; Pincherle 326; RV 578. Copyright by CASA RICORDI-BMG RICORDI S.p.A., Milan. Reprinted by permission.

b) Allegro (second movement)

20

78 VIVALDI Concerto Grosso, Op. 3, No. 2: II

B of ritornello

30

Vivaldi's collection of twelve concertos, *L'estro armonico* (The Harmonic Fancy, Op. 3, Amsterdam, 1711), established his European reputation. For the first Allegro of his solo concertos, Vivaldi adopted the alternation of ritornellos and solo episodes which characterized Torelli's fast movements. He also applied this structure, though more loosely, to the concerto grosso, in which the soloists were a group of players known as the *concertino* (little concerto) or small ensemble, as distinguished from the *concerto grosso* (big concerto), or large ensemble. Vivaldi's approach to the first Allegro is illustrated in the second movement of Op. 3, No. 2, RV 578.[1] Players of the concertino, made up of two violins and a cello, were designated in the score as "concertanti" (concertizing, or solo, players).

In the Adagio e spiccato (detached) (a), the soloists play in unison with the orchestra violins and cellos, except for two measures just before the close, when the solo violins are accompanied only by the violas. This movement is a study in chromatic harmony in which suspensions and other dissonances abound. Diminished-seventh chords appear several times, usually prepared by having the dissonant notes sounded in the previous chord, but in some instances (measures 9 and 12) not prepared at all, just as some seventh chords (measures 3 and 9) are not prepared. These previously unsanctioned usages are introduced with a freedom that even today strikes us as refreshing.

In the Allegro (b), the opening ritornello has three motivic sections—measures 14–16, 17–19, and 20–22—the last of which is an inverted counterpoint to the second. The three solo sections contain mostly figurative work, but in the second (measure 38) there is a veiled reference to the opening tutti motive. An unusual feature of this movement is that in the closing ritornello the order of motives is reversed. The final seven measures constitute an epilogue composed anew but based on the downward octave skip of the opening motive. This movement is also unusual in that only one of four main tutti, the third, is in a foreign key, D minor. Far from following a textbook plan, Vivaldi's Allegro structures show an infinity of invention.

---

1. There are several catalogues of Vivaldi's works. The most recent and reliable is known as "RV," Peter Ryom, *Verzeichnis der Werke Antonio Vivaldis: kleine Ausgabe* (Leipzig, 1974; suppl., Poitiers, 1979).

Antonio Vivaldi

Concerto for Violin, Op. 9, No. 2, RV 345

Largo (second movement)

Vivaldi, *La Cetra* (Amsterdam, 1728), ed. Gian Francesco Malipiero (Milan: Ricordi, 1952), 126:18–19.
F. I, 51; Pincherle 214; RV 345.

Taken from the collection *La Cetra* (The Kithara, 1728), this slow movement exhibits many features of the early Classic style: balanced phrases, and frequent half-cadences clarifying the structure, trills, triplets, and cadences softened by appoggiaturas. The slow, striking harmonic changes over the long dominant pedal (measures 122–125) intensify suspense after a choppy exposition. Like most of Vivaldi's slow movements, this one is lightly scored; only the solo cello and the continuo play with the solo violin.

80 JEAN-PHILIPPE RAMEAU (1683–1764)

Hippolyte et Aricie

Act IV, Scene 1: *Ah! faut-il*

Rameau, *Oeuvres complètes*, 6, ed. Vincent d'Indy (Paris: Durand, 1900), pp. 262–67.

Je ne ver_rai plus les beaux yeux Qui fai _ saient mon bon_heur su_pré _ _me.

Ah! faut-il, en un jour, per _ dre tout ce que j'ai _ me?

Et les maux que je crains, et les biens que je perds, Tout acca_ble mon cœur d'une douleur _ ex -

Ah! faut-il, en un jour, perdre tout ce que j'aime?
Et les maux que je crains, et les biens que je perds,
Tout accable mon coeur d'une douleur extrême.
Sous le nuage affreux dont mes jours sont couverts,
Que deviendra ma gloire aux yeux de l'univers?

Ah! faut-il, en un jour, perdre tout ce que j'aime?

Mon père pour jamais me bannit de ces lieux
Si chéris de Diane même.
Je ne verrai plus les beaux yeux
Qui faisaient mon bonheur suprême.

Ah, must I, in a day, lose all that I love?
And the troubles I fear, and the riches I lose,
all overwhelm my heart with extreme pain.
Under the terrible cloud that darkens my days,
what will become of my glory in the eyes of
  the world?
Ah, must I, in a day, lose all that I love?

My father is banishing me forever from these parts
so dear to Diane herself.
I shall see no more the beautiful eyes
which made me supremely happy.

—Simon-Joseph Pellegrin

Abbé S. J. de Pellegrin drew heavily on Racine's *Phèdre* for the libretto of this *tragédie lyrique*, first performed in Paris in 1733. Hyppolyte, falsely accused of violating his stepmother, complains in this monologue of his banishment and separation from his beloved Aricie.

The music illustrates how Rameau both remained faithful to the Lully tradition and departed from it. Like similar scenes by Lully, this one is a mixture of recitative and an aria-like refrain. After its melody is introduced in the opening orchestral tutti, the tuneful and measured refrain, "Ah! faut-il, en un jour, perdre tout ce que j'aime?" (Ah, must I, in a day, lose all that I love?), appears three times. The rest of the monologue—speechlike, with shorter notes per syllable and frequent changes of meter—lacks the qualities of well-formed melody. Rameau expressed Hippolyte's anguish with harmony highly charged with dissonances that propel it forward, as is evident from the number of sevenths, ninths, diminished fifths, and augmented fourths called for by the bass figures, and the obligatory appoggiaturas and other ornaments notated in the parts. Rameau replaced the five-part string orchestra of Lully with four-part strings, augmented by flutes, oboes, and bassoons.

JOHANN SEBASTIAN BACH (1685–1750)

Praeludium et Fuga in A Minor, BWV 543

Reprinted by permission of Bärenreiter-Verlag Kassel, Basel, Tours, London from: *Neue Ausgabe sämtlicher Werke,* Serie IV, *Orgel Werke,* Band 5, ed. Dietrich Kilian (Kassel, 1972), pp. 186–97.

During a stay in Weimar (1708–17), when Bach is believed to have composed this work, he copied out many concertos of Italian composers and made arrangements of some of them. Elements of the Italian concerto seep into a number of his toccatas and fugues, particularly in this Prelude and Fugue in A Minor. In the Prelude violinistic figuration resembling that of concerto solos alternates with toccata-like sections, including a pedal solo (measures 25–28), and chains of suspensions in the manner of Corelli (measures 37–38).

The structure of the fugue is analogous to that of a concerto Allegro. The opening exposition gives each of four "voices" a chance to state the violinistic subject on either the tonic minor or the dominant minor. The episode that follows, as well as others later on, has the character of solo sections, while the returns of the subject in related keys (E minor, C major, D minor) and in the tonic function like tuttis. Following the last statement of the subject (measures 131–36) there is an elaborate cadenza.

82 Johann Sebastian Bach

Durch Adams Fall, BWV 637

a) Chorale melody

b) Organ chorale

a) Text by Lazarus Spengler, *Geistliche Lieder auffs new gebossert* (Wittemberg: Joseph King, 1535), after Johannes Zahn, *Die Melodien der deutschen evangelischen Kirchenlieder* (Gütersloh, 1892), 4, No. 7549.

Durch Adams Fall is ganz verderbt
Menschlich Natur und Wesen;
Dasselb Gift ist auf uns geerbt,
Daß wir nicht mochten g'nesen
Ohn Gottes Trost, der uns erlöst
Hat von dem grossen Schaden,
Darein die Schlang' hienam bezwang
Gotts Zorn auf sich zu laden.
     —LAZARUS SPENGLER

Through Adam's fall are entirely spoiled
both human nature and character.
The same venom was by us inherited,
so that we could not recover from it
without God's solace, which saved us
from great harm;
for the serpent somehow managed
to take unto itself God's anger.

As in the other chorale preludes of the *Orgelbüchlein* (Little Organ Book), which Bach compiled mostly in Weimar (1716–17) but never finished, the chorale melody of *Durch Adams Fall* (Through Adam's fall) is heard once, in complete, continuous, and readily recognizable form. The tune itself (a) is in *Bar* form, consisting of a repeated section (two *Stollen*, each with two lines of text) and a closing section (*Abgesang* of four lines).

Bach's arrangement of the chorale *Durch Adams Fall* is one of his most graphic representations. A jagged series of dissonant leaps in the pedals depicts the idea of "fall," departing from a consonant chord and falling into a dissonant one—as if from innocence into sin—while the twisting chromatic lines in the inner voices suggest at once temptation, sorrow, and the sinuous writhing of the serpent.

83 JOHANN SEBASTIAN BACH

Cantata: *Wachet auf, ruft uns die Stimme,* BWV 140

1. Chorus: *Wachet auf*

Norton Critical Scores, from J. S. Bach, *Neue Ausgabe sämtlicher Werke*, Serie I, Band 27: *Kantaten zum 24. bis 27. Sonntag nach Trinitatis*, ed. Alfred Dürr (Kassel: Bärenreiter-Verlag, 1968). Reprinted by permission.

83 J.S. BACH Cantata, *Wachet auf,* BWV 140: I

Wachet auf, ruft uns die Stimme
Der Wächter sehr hoch auf der Zinne,
Wach auf, du Stadt Jerusalem!
Mitternacht heißt diese Stunde;
Sie rufen uns mit hellem Munde:
Wo seid ihr klugen Jungfrauen?
Wohl auf, der Bräutgam kömmt,
Steht auf, die Lampen nehmt!
Alleluja!
Macht euch bereit
Zu der Hochzeit,
Ihr müsset ihm entgegen gehn!
—Philipp Nicolai

"Wake up," calls the voice
of the watchmen, high up in the tower,
"wake up, O city of Jerusalem!"
Midnight is this hour;
they call us with loud mouths:
"Where are you, wise virgins?
Cheer up, the bridegroom comes;
get up, take your lamps!
Alleluia!
Make yourselves ready
for the wedding.
You must go to meet him."

2. Tenor Recitative: *Er kommt*

Er kommt, er kommt, der Bräutgam kommt!	He comes, he comes, the bridegroom comes!
Ihr Töchter Zions, kommt heraus,	You, daughters of Zion, come out.
Sein Ausgang eilet aus der Höhe	He is hurrying from on high
In euer Mutter Haus.	into your mother's house.
Der Bräutgam kommt, der einem Rehe	The bridegroom comes; like a roe
Und jungem Hirsche gleich	and a young hart
Auf denen Hügeln springt	leaping on the hills,
Und euch das Mahl der Hochzeit bringt.	he brings you the wedding feast.
Wacht auf, ermuntert euch!	Wake up, get yourselves up
Den Bräutgam zu empfangen!	to receive the bridegroom.
Dort, sehet, kommt er hergegangen.	There, see, he approaches.

3. Aria (Duet): *Wann kommst du, mein Heil?*

SEELE:	Wenn kömmst du, mein Heil?	SOUL:	When will you come, my salvation?
JESUS:	Ich komme, dein Teil.	JESUS:	I come, a part of yourself.
SEELE:	Ich warte mit brennendem Öle;	SOUL:	I wait with burning oil.
	Eröffne den Saal,		Open the hall
	Zum himmlischen Mahl,		to the heavenly feast!
JESUS:	Ich öffne den Saal,	JESUS:	I am opening the hall
	Zum himmlischen Mahl,		to the heavenly feast.
SEELE:	Komm, Jesu!	SOUL:	Come, Jesus!
JESUS:	Komm, liebliche Seele!	JESUS:	Come, lovely Soul!

4. Chorale: *Zion hört die Wächter singen*

83 J.S. BACH Cantata, *Wachet auf,* BWV 140: IV

Zion Hört die Wächter singen,
Das Herz tut ihr vor Freuden springen,
Sie wachet und steht eilend auf.
Ihr Freund kommt vom Himmel prächtig,
Von Gnaden stark, von Wahrheit mächtig,
Ihr Licht wird hell, ihr Stern geht auf.
Nun komm, du werte Kron,
Herr Jesu, Gottes Sohn!
Hosianna!
Wir folgen all zum Freudensaal
Und halten mit das Abendmahl.
—PHILIPP NICOLAI

Zion hears the watchmen singing;
her heart jumps for joy,
she wakes and gets up quickly.
Her friend comes from heaven proudly,
sturdy in grace, mighty in truth;
her light shines bright, her star is rising.
Now come, you worthy crown,
Lord Jesus, God's son.
Hosanna!
We all follow to the hall of joy
and join in the evening meal.

5. Recitative: *So geh herein zu mir*

So geh her-ein zu mir, du mir er-wähl-te Braut! Ich ha-be mich mit dir von

E-wig-keit ver-traut. Dich will ich auf mein Herz, auf mei-nen Arm gleich wie ein Sie-gel set-zen und

dein be-trüb-tes Aug er-göt-zen. Ver-giß, o See-le, nun die Angst, den Schmerz, den

du er-dul-den müs-sen; auf mei-ner Lin-ken sollst du ruhn, und mei-ne Rech-te soll dich küs-sen.

So geh herein zu mir,	So come in with me,
Du mir erwählte Braut!	My chosen bride!
Ich habe mich mit dir	I have bound myself
Von Ewigkeit vertraut.	to you for eternity!
Dich will ich auf mein Herz,	I will set you on my heart
Auf meinen Arm gleich wie ein Siegel setzen	and also on my arm as a seal
Und dein betrübtes Aug ergötzen.	and delight your sorry eye.
Vergiß, o Seele, nun	Forget now, O soul,
Die Angst, den Schmerz,	the anxiety, the pain
Den du erdulden müssen;	that you had to endure.
Auf meiner Linken sollst du ruhn,	On my left will you rest,
Une meine Rechte soll dich küssen.	and my right will kiss you.

6. Aria (Duet): *Mein Freund ist mein!*

83 J.S. BACH Cantata, *Wachet auf,* BWV 140:VI

83 J.S. BACH Cantata, *Wachet auf*, BWV 140:VI

11

Da capo *dal segno*

SEELE: Mein Freund ist mein,	SOUL: My friend is mine!
JESUS: Und ich bin sein,	JESUS: And I am his!
BEIDE: Die Liebe soll nichts scheiden;	BOTH: Nothing shall keep love apart;
SEELE: Ich will mit dir in Himmels Rosen weiden,	SOUL: I want to graze with with you in heaven's roses;
JESUS: Du sollst mit mir in Himmels Rosen weiden,	JESUS: You shall graze with me in heaven's roses;
BEIDE: Da Freude die Fülle, da Wonne wird sein.	BOTH: there fullness of joy, there bliss will reign.

7. Chorale: *Gloria sei dir gesungen*

Gloria sei dir gesungen
Mit Menschen- und englischen Zungen,
Mit Harfen und mit Zimbeln schon.
Von zwölf Perlen sind die Pforten
An deiner Stadt; wir sind Konsorten
Der Engel hoch um deinen Thron.
Kein Aug hat je gespürt,
Kein Ohr hat je gehört
Solche Freude.
Des sind wir froh,
Io io,
Ewig in dulci jubilo.
—PHILIPP NICOLAI

May the Gloria be sung to you
with people's and angels' tongues,
with harps and with cymbals too.
Of twelve pearls are the gates
to your city; we are consorts
of the angels high around your throne.
No eye has ever seen
nor ear has ever heard
such joy.
Of this we are happy,
Oho, oho!
Forever *in dulci jubilo.*

Wachet auf, first performed November 25, 1731, is one of the few cantatas of J. S. Bach that can be dated precisely. It was composed for the 27th Sunday after Trinity, which occurred only twice in Bach's Leipzig period—1731 and 1742—and various circumstances exclude 1742. The Gospel read at the Sunday service was Matthew 25:1–13, which tells of the ten virgins who watch by night for the arrival of the bridegroom. Some of the virgins are wise, because they brought oil for their lamps; the foolish ones, who are compelled to fetch some oil, miss his arrival and are locked out of the wedding hall. Three stanzas of Philipp Nicolai's chorale that dwell upon this parable serve as texts for the opening chorus, a chorale movement for the tenors, and the final chorus. The remaining poetry by an unknown author, for the recitatives and arias, is based on the same Gospel account. As he often did, Bach arranged the seven movements in a symmetrical fashion: the middle tenor-chorale stanza is flanked by a recitative and aria on each side, and chorale-choruses begin and end the cantata.

The opening chorus, the weightiest movement in Bach's chorale cantatas, is one of the most magnificent of them all. Its form is modeled on the ritornello structure of the instrumental concerto. The full sixteen-measure ritornello returns twice: between the two *Stollen* (lines 1–3 and 4–6) of the chorale and at the end. An abridged ritornello (omitting the first four bars) precedes the *Abgesang* (lines 7–12). As in many Vivaldi concertos, the ritornello is divisible into four-bar phrases based on several distinct motives. The first three notes of the chorale together with its verbal message inspired the musical motives of the ritornello. The twelve dotted-chord patterns of the first phrase (motive a) suggest a church bell striking midnight. The rising motive (b) in the violins and oboe (measures 4–7), which hesitates at the third and fifth of the triad, alludes to the first three notes of the chorale but also to the anxiety and expectancy of the virgins. The rushing rising figure in the first violins (measure 9, motive c) suggests the vigilance and impatience of the wise virgins. The last four measures of the ritornello combine motives a (in the continuo), b (in the oboes), and c (in the first violins). The instrumental accompaniment of the chorale phrases rework these motives, while the chorale melody, sung only by the sopranos, supplies subjects for the imitative counterpoint of the three other voices. Only on the word "Alleluja" (measures 135ff.) do the voices pick up one of the instrumental motives, c, which is forged into a fugue subject.

The first recitative (Number 2), accompanied by continuo only, typifies Bach's approach in its triadic and often wide leaps, their tension heightened by the dissonant chords they outline. The second recitative (Number 5), sung by the bridegroom who represents Christ, is accompanied by strings, as the speeches of Jesus are in Bach's Passions.

Both arias are duets. *Wann kommst du, mein Heil?* (When will you come, my salvation?; Number 3) is a conversation between the Soul and Jesus written as a love duet. The arabesques woven around the voices by the violino piccolo (a three-quarter size violin specially tuned to make playing high notes easier) brings to mind the improvisatory passage work that embellished the simple lines of Corelli's slow movements (see facsimile in HWM, p. 377). At the end of the aria, performers repeat only the opening ritornello instead of a full da capo.

The other aria-duet, *Mein Freund ist mein* (My friend is mine, Number 6), by contrast, is a full-blown da capo form. It is also more conventional in that the ritornello announces the melody that the voices then elaborate. This melody is in the *galant* style of the 1730s, made up of balanced two-measure phrases. It expresses the contentment of a love union in the parallel phrases sung by the two voices and in their parallel motion in thirds (for example, measures 8–12). In the middle section, which reworks the same material, this oneness is symbolized by quasi-canonic writing. The runs that had been the preserve of the oboe are commandeered by the singers to portray the grazing in heaven's roses. The da capo ends at the fermata (measure 46).

The central chorale (Number 4) is one of the best-known pieces of Bach, who must have been fond of it too because he transcribed it for organ (BWV 645), and Johann Georg Schübler published it as the first of *Sechs*

Choräle von verschiedener Art (Six Chorales of Diverse Sorts, ca. 1748–49). As in the aria just discussed, Bach composed the obbligato line (here played by strings) in the modern style. We hear an opening two-measure phrase that is immediately repeated and is then followed by another pair of two-measure phrases, the second of which joins even shorter segments. All of these phrases end—in comic-opera fashion—on a weak beat. But despite the stops and starts, a remarkable continuity rules, and the violins project a single affection of quiet joy against the disparate lines of the chorale's second stanza sung by the tenor section.

Compared to the chorale in Number 4, the note values of the tune are doubled in the final chorus (Number 7), permitting Bach to energize the hymn with driving quarter notes in the bass and elsewhere. The entire orchestra joins in this number, playing *colla parte*—that is, doubling the vocal parts.

JOHANN SEBASTIAN BACH
Mass in B Minor, BWV 232

Credo: *Symbolum Nicenum*

a) Et in Spiritum sanctum Dominum

Reprinted by permission of Bärenreiter-Verlag Kassel, Basel, Tours, London from J. S. Bach, *Neue Ausgabe sämtlicher Werke*, ed. Friedrich Smend (Kassel, 1954), pp. 190–215.

b) Confiteor

17

c) Et expecto resurrectionem

For a translation of the Credo, see NAWM 49.

Bach assembled the Mass in B Minor between around 1747 and 1749, mostly from previously composed music. Several of the movements were choruses from cantatas, in which the German text was replaced by the Latin words of the Mass and the music sometimes reworked. One of these is the *Et expecto* (c), taken from Cantata No. 120 (*Gott, man lobet dich in der Stille,* 1728–29). The Et in Spiritum (a) and Confiteor (b) date from 1747–49. The entire work was apparently never performed in Bach's lifetime.

Et in Spiritum sanctum (a), for bass solo with two oboi d'amore, like a number of other late works of Bach, shows traces of the popular *galant* style—repeated phrases, parallel thirds, and slow harmonic rhythm. A further modern trait is the great care Bach took to subordinate the instrumental parts to the voice, indicating *piano* for the obbligato instruments when the voice is singing and *forte* when it is not. This aria is singularly monothematic, with the instrumental ritornello and vocal elaboration sharing the same material. The pillars of the structure are three full statements of the twelve-measure ritornello, in A major, E major, then again in A major. The sometimes awkward text-setting suggests that the music may originally have been composed for other words.

The Confiteor (b), on the other hand, must have been expressly set to this text. As in the opening of the Credo, Bach here took the appropriate segment from the Gregorian Credo II (*Liber usualis,* p. 67) as a cantus firmus (it is heard in the tenor part starting at measure 73). He wrote the choral parts in *stile antico,* marked by the *alla breve* time signature and fugal procedures of that style. But in the continuo accompaniment he added a modern touch: a quasi-ostinato bass. At the words "Et expecto resurrectionem mortuorum" (And I await the resurrection of the dead), Bach dropped the cantus firmus and inserted a transitional Adagio, intensely chromatic and dissonant, symbolizing the death that will be defied by the resurrection.

The brilliant Vivace e Allegro that follows, triumphantly reiterating the words "Et expecto resurrectionem mortuorum" (c), is a reworking of the chorus *Jauchzet, ihr erfreuten Stimmen* (Shout, you joyful voices), from Cantata No. 120. Some of the purely instrumental music of the cantata chorus is ingeniously made to accompany a choral fugue (measures 61–87).

85 GEORGE FRIDERIC HANDEL (1685–1759)
Giulio Cesare: Act III, Scene 4: Dall'ondoso periglio

Handel, *Werke,* Ausgabe der deutschen Händelgesellschaft, ed. Friedrich W. Chrysander (Leipzig: Breitkopf and Härtel, 1875), 68: 102–8.

Dall'ondoso periglio	From the perilous sea
Salvo mi porta al lido	safely takes me to the beach,
Il mio propizio fato.	my propitious destiny.
Quì la celeste parca	Here heavenly fate
Non tronca ancor lo stame a la mia vita!	does not yet cut the thread of my life.
Mà dove andrò e chi mi porge aita?	But where shall I go and who will come to my aid?
Ove son le mie schiere?	Where are my ranks?
Ove son le legioni,	Where are my legions,
Che a tante mie vittorie il varco apriro?	that to so many victories opened the way?
Solo in queste erme arene	In these solitary arenas
Al monarca del mondo errar conviene?	only the King of the World is at home.
Aure, aure, deh, per pietà	Breezes, for pity's sake,
Spirate al petto mio,	breathe on my breast
Per dar conforto, oh Dio!	to comfort me, O God,
Al mio dolor.	in my pain.
Dite, dite dov'è che fà	Tell me, where is she,
L'idolo del mio sen,	where is the idol of my heart,
L'amato e dolce ben	beloved and sweet object
Di questo cor.	of this heart.
Mà d'ogni intorno i' veggio	But all around me I see,
Sparse d'arme e d'estinti	strewn with weapons and corpses,
L'infortuna arene,	this unfortunate arena,
Segno d'infausto annunzio al fin sarà.	an ill omen of my end.

—NICOLA HAYM

Handel composed about forty operas for London between 1711 and 1741. *Giulio Cesare*, on a libretto by Nicola Haym (1679–1729), was produced in 1724 when Handel was enjoying his greatest success as an opera composer.

In this scene Caesar finds himself on a deserted shore, to which he swam to escape enemy troops. The scene begins with a ritornello describing the sea breezes that Caesar will address in his aria, but it is interrupted by a recitative with string accompaniment, "Dall'ondoso periglio" (From the perilous sea). Here Caesar takes stock of his situation, excitedly asking, "Where shall I go? Who will come to my aid? Where are my ranks?" (measures 29–34). Each question is punctuated by dotted figures, like distorted dissonant fanfares, in the strings. This *recitativo obbligato*, as the orchestrally accompanied recitative was then called, exploits emphatic inverted seventh chords and diminished-seventh chords—sonorities then still fresh to the ear—with great dramatic effect.

Caesar begins his aria unaccompanied. Then we hear the ritornello momentarily before he continues *Aure, deh per pietà* (Breezes, for pity's sake), each three-measure phrase interrupted by the breeze music. After a deceptive cadence and then a renewed close on the dominant, the first stanza of the aria is reviewed, but with more continuous and stirring development of the themes presented piecemeal earlier. The middle section, in minor, begins with the same downward leap of the fifth that began the aria. With clipped phrases, lightly accompanied, Caesar implores the breezes to tell him the fate of his beloved Cleopatra. Once again he is interrupted. The listener now expects the da capo repetition, but accompanied recitative breaks in as Caesar expresses the helplessness of his situation. Only then do we hear the da capo (written out in the score). By scrambling the conventional order of musical events slightly, Handel achieved actuality, atmosphere, and suspense. The unusual form of this scene may be represented in this diagram:

Ritornello	Recitativo obbligato	Aria A^1		Rit.	Aria A^2		Rit.	Aria B		Recitativo obbligato	Aria da capo	
F				C			F	d		D	B♭	F
1	23	42		73	77		98	105		124	130 131	190

GEORGE FRIDERIC HANDEL

Jephtha: Act II, Chorus

How dark, O Lord, are Thy decrees!

Handel, *Werke*, Ausgabe der deutschen Händelgesellschaft, ed. Friedrich W. Chrysander (Leipzig, 1858–1902), 44:174–87.

86 HANDEL *Jephtha*

86 HANDEL *Jephtha*

89 *A tempo ordinario.*

No cer_tain bliss, no so_lid peace, we mor_tals know,___ on earth___ be-

No cer_tain bliss, no so_-lid

93

_low; we mor_tals know,___ on earth___ be_low, on earth be_low,

peace, no so_lid peace,

we mor_tals know,___ on earth___ be_

No cer_tain bliss, no so_lid peace, no cer_tain bliss, no so_lid

No cer_tain bliss, no so_

Jephtha, on a libretto by Thomas Morell, was Handel's last oratorio. It was first performed at Covent Garden, London, on February 26, 1752.

Like the choruses of Greek tragedy, this chorus voices the sorrow and dismay of a people—the Israelites, and by extension of the spectators—on the predicament of Jephtha, who is forced by a vow to sacrifice his own daughter (see the commentary on NAWM 64). It is divided into four sections. Ominous chords in the strings in an unrelenting dotted rhythm intro-

duce and accompany the opening words. The first voice to enter braves a
leap of a minor sixth, while the others imitate with easier intervals, after
which the chorus continues homophonically. A canonic section, marked
Larghetto, on a theme full of wide skips sets the words "All our joys to sorrow turning." A tense fugue follows on a subject derived from a Mass by
Frantisek Habermann, from whom Handel also borrowed other motives for
this oratorio. One moment midway in the fugue strikingly resembles the "Et
in terra pax" of Habermann's Gloria:

Handel

Habermann

The last section is a Larghetto in triple time on the text "Yet on this
maxim still obey, whatever is, is right." The admonition to obey is set in
fugal style, as one would expect, but the maxim itself is punctuated by an
astonishing unison orchestral figure that separates the lonely, exposed, fatal-
istic unison statements of "whatever is," and the unquestioning, dogmatic
choral response "is right." The alternation of admonition and maxim, of fate
and law, is taken from C minor through a round of modulations to return
inexorably to a pessimistic C minor.

Diminished intervals and chromaticism are prominent throughout this
expression of anguish and fatalism, one of Handel's greatest choruses and
one of his last acts of composition before his eyesight failed.

INSTRUMENT NAMES
AND ABBREVIATIONS

The following tables set forth the English, Italian, German, and French names used for the various musical instruments in these scores, and their respective abbreviations.

WOODWINDS

English	Italian	German	French
Piccolo (Picc.)	Flauto piccolo (Fl. Picc.)	Kleine Flöte (Kl. Fl.)	Petite flûte
Flute (Fl.)	Flauto (Fl.); Flauto grande (Fl. gr.)	Große Flöte (Fl. gr.)	Flûte (Fl.)
Alto flute	Flauto contralto (fl.c–alto)	Altflöte	Flûte en sol
Oboe (Ob.)	Oboe (Ob.)	Hoboe (Hb.); Oboe (Ob.)	Hautbois (Hb.)
English horn (E.H.)	Corno inglese (C. or Cor. ingl., C.i.)	Englisches Horn	Cor anglais (C.A.)
Sopranino clarinet	Clarinetto piccolo (clar. picc.)		
Clarinet (C., Cl., Clt., Clar.)	Clarinetto (Cl., Clar.)	Klarinette (Kl.)	Clarinette (Cl.)
Bass clarinet (B. Cl.)	Clarinetto basso (Cl. b., Cl. basso, Clar. basso)	Bass Klarinette (Bkl.)	Clarinette basse (Cl. bs.)
Bassoon (Bsn., Bssn.)	Fagotto (Fag,. Fg.)	Fagott (Fag., Fg.)	Basson (Bssn.)
Contrabassoon (C. Bsn.)	Contrafagotto (Cfg., C. Fag., Cont. F.)	Kontrafagott (Kfg.)	Contrebasson (C. bssn.)

BRASS

English	Italian	German	French
French horn (Hr., Hn.)	Corno (Cor., C.)	Horn (Hr.) [pl. Hörner (Hrn.)]	Cor; Cor à pistons
Trumpet (Tpt., Trpt., Trp., Tr.)	Tromba (Tr.)	Trompete (Tr., Trp.)	Trompette (Tr.)
Trumpet in D	Tromba piccola (Tr. picc.)		
Cornet	Cornetta	Kornett	Cornet à pistons (C. à p., Pist.)
Trombone (Tr., Tbe., Trb., Trm., Trbe.)	Trombone [pl. Tromboni (Tbni., Trni.)]	Posaune (Ps., Pos.)	Trombone (Tr.)
Tuba (Tb.)	Tuba (Tb., Tba.)	Tuba (Tb.)	Tuba (Tb.)

PERCUSSION

English	Italian	German	French
Percussion (Perc.)	Percussione	Schlagzeug (Schlag.)	Batterie (Batt.)
Kettledrums (K. D.)	Timpani (Timp., Tp.)	Pauken (Pk.)	Timbales (Timb.)
Snare drum (S. D.)	Tamburo piccolo (Tamb. picc.)	Kleine Trommel (Kl. Tr.)	Caisse claire (C. cl.), Caisse roulante
	Tamburo militare (Tamb. milit.)		Tambour militaire (Tamb. milit.)
Bass drum (B. drum)	Gran cassa (Gr. Cassa, Gr. C., G. C.)	Große Trommel (Gr. Tr.)	Grosse caisse (Gr. c.)
Cymbals (Cym., Cymb.)	Piatti (P., Ptti., Piat.)	Becken (Beck.)	Cymbales (Cym.)
Tam-Tam (Tam-T.)			
Tambourine (Tamb.)	Tamburino (Tamb.)	Schellentrommel, Tamburin	Tambour de Basque (T. de B., Tamb. de Basque)
Triangle (Trgl., Tri.)	Triangolo (Trgl.)	Triangel	Triangle (Triang.)
Glockenspiel (Glocken.)	Campanelli (Cmp.)	Glockenspiel	Carillon
Bells (Chimes)	Campane (Cmp.)	Glocken	Cloches
Antique Cymbals	Crotali, Piatti antichi	Antiken Zimbeln	Cymbales antiques
Sleigh Bells	Sonagli (Son.)	Schellen	Grelots
Xylophone (Xyl.)	Xilofono	Xylophon	Xylophone

STRINGS

English	Italian	German	French
Violin (V., Vl., Vn., Vln., Vi.)	Violino (V., Vl., Vln.)	Violine (V., Vl., Vln.) Geige (Gg.)	Violon (V., Vl., Vln.)
Viola (Va., Vl., *pl.* Vas.)	Viola (Va., Vla.) *pl.* Viole (Vle.)	Bratsche (Br.)	Alto (A.)
Violoncello, Cello (Vcl., Vc.)	Violoncello (Vc., Vlc., Vcllo.)	Violoncell (Vc., Vlc.)	Violoncelle (Vc.)
Double bass (D. Bs.)	Contrabasso (Cb., C. B.) *pl.* Contrabassi or Bassi (C. Bassi, Bi.)	Kontrabass (Kb.)	Contrebasse (C. B.)

OTHER INSTRUMENTS

English	Italian	German	French
Harp (Hp., Hrp.)	Arpa (A., Arp.)	Harfe (Hrf.)	Harpe (Hp.)
Piano	Pianoforte (P.-f., Pft.)	Klavier	Piano
Celesta (Cel.)			
Harpsichord	Cembalo	Cembalo	Clavecin
Harmonium (Harmon.)			
Organ (Org.)	Organo	Orgel	Orgue
Guitar		Gitarre (Git.)	
Mandoline (Mand.)			

GLOSSARY

a The phrases *a 2, a 3* (etc.) indicate that the part is to be played in unison by 2, 3 (etc.) players; when a simple number (1., 2., etc.) is placed over a part, it indicates that only the first (second, etc.) player in that group should play.

abdämpfen To mute.

aber But.

accelerando (acc.) Growing faster.

accompagnato (accomp.) In a continuo part, this indicates that the chord-playing instrument resumes (*cf. tasto solo*).

adagio Slow, leisurely.

a demi-jeu Half-organ; i.e., softer registration.

ad libitum (ad lib.) An indication giving the performer liberty to: (1) vary from strict tempo; (2) include or omit the part of some voice or instrument; (3) include a cadenza of his own invention.

agitato Agitated, excited.

alla breve A time signature (¢) indicating, in the sixteenth century, a single breve per two-beat measure; in later music, the half note rather than the quarter is the unit of beat.

allargando (allarg.) Growing broader.

alle, alles All, every, each.

allegretto A moderately fast tempo (between allegro and andante).

allegro A rapid tempo (between allegretto and presto).

alto, altus (A.) The deeper of the two main divisions of women's (or boys') voices.

am Frosch At the heel (of a bow).

am Griffbrett Play near, or above, the fingerboard of a string instrument.

amoroso Loving, amorous.

am Steg On the bridge (of an instrument).

ancora Again.

andante A moderately slow tempo (between adagio and allegretto).

animato, animé Animated.

a piacere The execution of the passage is left to the performer's discretion.

arco Played with the bow.

arpeggiando, arpeggiato (arpeg.) Played in harp style, i.e., the notes of the chord played in quick succession rather than simultaneously.

assai Very.

a tempo At the (basic) tempo.

attacca Begin what follows without pausing.

auf dem On the (as in *auf dem G,* on the G string).

Auftritt Scene.

Ausdruck Expression.

ausdrucksvoll With expression.

Auszug Arrangement.

baguettes Drumsticks (*baguettes de bois, baguettes timbales de bois,* wooden drumsticks or kettledrum sticks; *baguettes d'éponge,* sponge-headed drumsticks; *baguettes midures,* semi-hard drumsticks; *baguettes dures,* hard drumsticks; *baguettes timbales en feutre,* felt-headed kettledrum sticks).

bariton Brass instrument.

bass, basso, bassus (B.) The lowest male voice.

Begleitung Accompaniment.

belebt Animated.

beruhigen To calm, to quiet.

bewegt Agitated.

bewegter More agitated.

bien Very.

breit Broadly.

breiter More broadly.

Bühne Stage.

cadenza An extended passage for solo instrument in free, improvisatory style.

calando Diminishing in volume and speed.

cambiare To change.

cantabile (cant.) In a singing style.

cantando In a singing manner.

canto Voice (as in *col canto,* a direction for the accompaniment to follow the solo part in tempo and expression).

cantus An older designation for the highest part in a vocal work.

chiuso Stopped, in horn playing.

col, colla, coll' With the.

come prima, come sopra As at first; as previously.

comme Like, as.

comodo Comfortable, easy.

con With

Continuo (Con.) A method of indicating an accompanying part by the bass notes only, together with figures designating the chords to be played above them. In general practice, the chords are played on a lute, harpsichord or organ, while, often, a viola da gamba or cello doubles the bass notes.

contratenor In earlier music, the name given to the third voice part which was added to the basic two-voice texture of discant and tenor, having the same range as the tenor which it frequently crosses.

corda String; for example, *seconda* (2*a*) *corda* is the second string (the A string on the violin).

coro Chorus.

coryphée Leader of a ballet or chorus.

countertenor Male alto, derived from *contratenor altus*.

crescendo (cresc.) Increasing in volume.

da capo (D.C.) Repeat from the beginning, usually up to the indication *Fine* (end).

daher From there.

dal segno Repeat from the sign.

Dämpfer (Dpf.) Mute.

decrescendo (decresc., decr.) Decreasing in volume.

delicato Delicate, soft.

dessus Treble.

détaché With a broad, vigorous bow stroke, each note bowed singly.

deutlich Distinctly.

diminuendo, diminuer (dim., dimin.) Decreasing in volume.

discantus Improvised counterpoint to an existing melody.

divisés, divisi (div.) Divided; indicates that the instrumental group should be divided into two or more parts to play the passage in question.

dolce Sweet and soft.

dolcemente Sweetly.

dolcissimo (dolciss.) Very sweet.

Doppelgriff Double stop.

doppelt Twice.

doppio movimento Twice as fast.

doux Sweet.

drängend Pressing on.

e And.

Echoton Like an echo.

éclatant Sparkling, brilliant.

einleiten To lead into.

Encore Again.

en dehors Emphasized.

en fusée Dissolving in.

erschütterung A violent shaking, deep emotion.

espressione intensa Intense expression.

espressivo (espress., espr.) Expressive.

et And.

etwas Somewhat, rather.

expressif (express.) Expressive.

falsetto Male singing voice in which notes above the ordinary range are obtained artificially.

falsobordone Four-part harmonization of psalm tones with mainly root-position chords.

fauxbourdon (faulx bourdon) Three-part harmony in which the chant melody in the treble is accompanied by two lower voices, one in parallel sixths, and the other improvised a fourth below the melody.

fermer brusquement To close abruptly.

fine End, close.

flatterzunge, flutter-tongue A special tonguing technique for wind intruments, producing a rapid trill-like sound.

flüchtig Fleeting, transient.

fois Time (as in *premier fois,* first time).

forte (f) Loud.

fortissimo (ff) Very loud (*fff* indicates a still louder dynamic).

fortsetzend Continuing.

forza Force.

frei Free.

fugato A section of a composition fugally treated.

funebre Funereal, mournful.

fuoco Fire, spirit.

furioso Furious.

ganz Entirely, altogether.

gebrochen Broken.

gedehnt Held back.

gemächlich Comfortable.

Generalpause (G.P.) Rest for the complete orchestra.

geschlagen Struck.

geschwinder More rapid, swift.

gesprochen Spoken.

gesteigert Intensified.

gestopft (chiuso) Stopped; for the notes of a horn obtained by placing the hand in the bell.

gestrichen (gestr.) Bowed.

gesungen Sung.

geteilt (get.) Divided; indicates that the instrumental group should be divided into two parts to play the passage in question.

gewöhnlich (gew., gewöhnl.)   Usual, customary.

giusto   Moderate.

gleichmässig   Equal, symmetrical.

gli altri   The others.

glissando (gliss.)   Rapidly gliding over strings or keys, producing a scale run.

grande   Large, great.

grave   Slow, solemn; deep, low.

gravement   Gravely, solemnly.

grazioso   Graceful.

groß, großes, großer, etc.   Large, big.

H⁻   *Hauptstimme,* the most important voice in the texture.

Halbe   Half.

Halt   Stop, hold.

harmonic (harm.)   A flute-like sound produced on a string instrument by lightly touching the string with the finger instead of pressing it down.

Hauptzeitmass   Original tempo.

heftiger   More passionate, violent.

hervortretend   Prominently.

Holz   Woodwinds.

hörbar   Audible.

immer   Always.

impetuoso   Impetuous, violent.

istesso tempo   The same tempo, as when the duration of the beat remains unaltered despite meter change.

klagend   Lamenting.

klangvoll   Sonorous, full-sounding.

klingen lassen   Allow to sound.

kräftig   Stong, forceful.

kurz   Short.

kurzer   Shorter.

laissez vibrer   Let vibrate; an indication to the player of a harp, cymbal, etc., that the sound must not be damped.

langsam   Slow.

langsamer   Slower.

largamente   Broadly.

larghetto   Slightly faster than largo.

largo   A very slow tempo.

lebhaft   Lively.

legato   Performed without any perceptible interruption between notes.

leggéro, leggiero (legg.)   Light and graceful.

legno   The wood of the bow (*col legno tratto,* bowed with the wood; *col legno battuto,* tapped with the wood; *col legno gestrich,* played with the wood).

leidenschaftlich   Passionate, vehement.

lent   Slow.

lentamente   Slowly.

lento   A slow tempo (between andante and largo).

l.h.   Abbreviation for "left hand."

lié   Tied.

ma   But.

maestoso   Majestic.

maggiore   Major key.

main   Hand (*droite,* right; *gauche,* left).

marcatissimo (marcatiss.)   With very marked emphasis.

marcato (mar.)   Marked, with emphasis.

marcia   March.

marqué   Marked, with emphasis.

mässig   Moderate.

mean   Middle part of a polyphonic composition.

meno   Less.

mezza voce   With half the voice power.

mezzo forte (mf)   Moderately loud.

mezzo piano (mp)   Moderately soft.

minore   In the minor mode.

minuetto   Minuet.

mit   With.

M.M.   Metronome; followed by an indication of the setting for the correct temp.

moderato, modéré   At a moderate tempo.

molto   Very, much.

mosso   Rapid.

motetus   In medieval polyphonic music, a voice part above the tenor; generally, the first additional part to be composed.

moto   Motion.

muta, mutano   Change the tuning of the instrument as specified.

N⁻   *Nebenstimme,* the second most important voice in the texture.

Nachslag   Auxiliary note (at end of trill).

nehmen (nimmt)   To take.

neue   New.

nicht, non   Not.

noch   Still, yet.

octava (okt., 8va)   Octave; if not otherwise qualified, means the notes marked should be played an octave higher than written.

ohne (o.)   Without.

open   In brass instruments, the opposite of muted. In string instruments, refers to the unstopped string (i.e., sounding at its full length).

ordinario, ordinairement (ordin., ord.)   In the usual way (generally cancelling an instruction to play using some special technique).

ôtez les sourdines   Remove the mutes.

parlando   A singing style with the voice approximating speech.

parte   Part (*colla parte,* the accompaniment is to follow the voice parts).

passione   Passion.

pause   Rest.

pedal (ped., P.)   In piano music, indicates that the damper pedal should be depressed; an asterisk indicates the point of release (brackets below the music are also used to indicate pedalling). On an organ, the pedals are a keyboard played with the feet.

perdendosi   Gradually dying away.

peu   Little, a little.

pianissimo (pp)   Very soft (*ppp* indicates a still softer dynamic).

piano (p)   Soft.

più   More.

pizzicato (pizz.)   The string plucked with the finger.

plötzlich   Suddenly, immediately.

plus   More.

pochissimo (pochiss.)   Very little.

poco   Little, a little.

poco a poco   Little by little.

ponticello (pont.)   The bridge (of a string instrument).

portato   Performance manner between legato and staccato.

prenez   Take up.

près de la table   On the harp, the plucking of the strings near the soundboard.

prestissimo   Very fast.

presto   A very quick tempo (faster than allegro).

prima   First.

principale (pr.)   Principal, solo.

quasi   Almost, as if.

quasi niente   Almost nothing, i.e., as softly as possible.

quintus   An older disignation for the fifth part in a vocal work.

rallentando (rall., rallent.)   Growing slower.

rasch   Quick.

recitative (recit.)   A vocal style designed to imitate and emphasize the natural inflections of speech.

rinforzando (rinf.)   Sudden accent on a single note or chord.

ritardando (rit., ritard.)   Gradually slackening in speed.

ritmico   Rhythmical.

rubato   A certain elasticity and flexibility of tempo, speeding up and slowing down, according to the requirements of the music.

ruhig   Calm.

ruhiger   More calmly.

saltando (salt.)   An indication to the string player to bounce the bow off the string by playing with short, quick bow-strokes.

sans   Without.

scherzando (scherz.)   Playfully.

schleppend   Dragging.

schnell   Fast.

schneller   Faster.

schon   Already.

schwerer   Heavier, more difficult.

schwermütig   Dejected, sad.

sec., secco   Dry, simple.

segno   Sign in form of *.𝄋.* indicating the beginning and end of a section to be repeated.

segue   (1) Continue to the next movement without pausing; (2) continue in the same manner.

sehr   Very.

semplice   Simple, in a simple manner.

sempre   Always, continually.

senza   Without.

senza mis[ura]   Free of regular meter.

serpent   Bass of the cornett family.

seulement   Only.

sforzando, sforzato (sfz, sf)   With sudden emphasis.

simile   In a similar manner.

sino al . . .   Up to the . . . (usually followed by a new tempo marking, or by a dotted line indicating a terminal point).

sombre   Dark, somber.

son   Sound.

sonore   Sonorous, with full tone.

sopra   Above; in piano music, used to indicate that one hand must pass above the other.

soprano (Sop., S.)   The voice with the highest range.

sordino (sord.)   Mute.

sostenendo, sostenuto (sost.)   Sustained.

sotto voce   In an undertone, subdued, under the breath.

sourdine   Mute.

soutenu   Sustained.

spiccato   With a light bouncing motion of the bow.

spirito   Spirited, lively.

spiritoso   Humorous.

sprechstimme (sprechst.)   Speaking voice.

staccato (stacc.)   Detached, separated, abruptly disconnected.

stentando, stentato (stent.)   Hesitating, retarding.

Stimme   Voice.

strepitoso, strepito   Noisy, boisterous.

stretto   In a non-fugal composition, indicates a concluding section at an increased speed.

stringendo (string.)   Quickening.

subito (sub.)   Suddenly, immediately.

sul   On the (as in *sul G.* on the G string).

suono   Sound, tone.

superius   The uppermost part.

sur   On.

Takt   Bar, beat.

tasto solo   In a continuo part, this indicates that only the string instrument plays; the chord-playing instrument is silent.

temp primo (temp I)   At the original tempo.

tendrement   Tenderly.

tenerezza   Tenderness.

tenor, tenore (T., ten.)   High male voice or part.

tenuto (ten.)   Held, sustained.

touche   Fingerboard or fret (of a string instrument).

tranquillo   Quiet, calm.

trauernd   Mournfully.

treble   Soprano voice or range.

tremolo (trem)   On string instruments, a quick reiteration of the same tone, produced by a rapid up-and-down movement of the bow; also a rapid alternation between two different notes.

très   Very.

trill (tr.)   The rapid alternation of a given note with the note above it. In a drum part it indicates rapid alternating strokes with two drumsticks.

triplum   In medieval polyphonic music, a voice part above the tenor.

tristement   Sadly.

troppo   Too much.

tutti   Literally, "all"; usually means all the instruments in a given category as distinct from a solo part.

übertönend   Drowning out.

unison (unis.)   The same notes or melody played by several instruments at the same pitch. Often used to emphasize that a phrase is not to be divided among several players.

Unterbrechung   Interruption, suspension.

veloce   Fast.

verhalten   Restrained, held back.

verklingen lassen   To let die away.

Verwandlung   Change of scene.

verzweiflungsvoll   Full of despair.

vibrato   Slight fluctuation of pitch around a sustained tone.

vif   Lively.

vigoroso   Vigorous, strong.

vivace   Quick, lively.

voce   Voice.

volti   Turn over (the page).

Vorhang auf   Curtain up.

Vorhang fällt, Vorhang zu   Curtain down.

voriges   Preceding.

vorwärts   Forward, onward.

weg   Away, beyond.

wieder   Again.

wie oben   As above, as before.

zart   Tenderly, delicately.

ziemlich   Suitable, fit.

zurückhaltend   Slackening in speed.

zurückkehrend zum   Return to, go back to.

Index of Composers

INDEX OF TITLES

INDEX OF FORMS AND GENRES

Index to NAWM References in Grout/Palisca, *A History of Western Music*, 5th Edition

KINGDOM WORKS